# Creating
# The Person

# Creating The Person

## A Practical Guide to the Development of Self

### By
### Inayat Khan

**OMEGA PUBLICATIONS**
NEW LEBANON

CREATING THE PERSON
First published September, 1995.

Cover design by Barkat Curtin and Abi'l-Khayr.
Printed by McNaughton & Gunn in the U.S.A.

ISBN 0-930872-51-7

OMEGA PUBLICATIONS
256 DARROW ROAD
NEW LEBANON NY 12125-9801

# Contents

# *Preface*

There is an old proverb that the place where two rivers meet is a place of heightened blessing. Pir-o-Murshid Hazrat Inayat Khan reminds me of this saying, representing as he does the confluence of two rivers of being, eastern and western. Born in India, Inayat Khan (1882-1927) was a brilliant musician and a student of a highly respected Sufi murshid (teacher) in Hyderabad, named Abu Hashim Madani. When he was dying, Murshid Madani called Inayat Khan to him and asked him to take his music to the West to harmonize East and West. In 1910 Inayat Khan set sail from India to New York. His music there, and later in Europe, took the form not only of vina recitals and voice concerts, but also of lectures on various themes of relevance to our times.

*Creating the Person* is one such theme. This series of twenty-three lectures was given in the summer of 1923 in Suresnes, a suburb of Paris, France, where Inayat Khan had settled with his American wife and four children. These lectures are the work of an artist, a musician, who offers a technique, one might say, for creating what he calls the greatest work of art: the human personality. We have here an introduction to a range of important qualities necessary for a developed personality. Each lecture focuses on one of these qualities, which include, among others, will power, gratitude, spiritual economy, gentleness, consideration, and justice.

Questions and answers have been included following each lecture, opening up the scope of discussion still further, since the contents of these questions and answers do not strictly adhere to the subject addressed in the lecture. In fact, the material contained in these questions and answers can be quite challenging. In the story of Harish Chandra, for example, one may wonder if the king might not have found some way to pay the tax for his son's cremation. Perhaps the story is symbolic, illustrative of firm adherence to a particular ideal, despite the most adverse of circumstances. This challenge to our thinking, then, becomes a means for progressing beyond our ordinary assessment of things. We need not be concerned, however, if we do not agree with all that Inayat Khan has to say about creating the person. He himself urged that if something was helpful, use it; otherwise, leave it alone.

What is unique about this series is that it provides direction for developing these qualities in one's everyday life. Inayat Khan calls this direction "ear-training," and he provides many brief and extended examples throughout these talks to help develop this ear-training. This orientation is welcome, even refreshing, because it is not dogmatic. "No principle must be blindly followed," he says. Rather, he affords us a design of the person, which may be filled in by us as we like, just as in Indian music the raga is improvised upon by the musician. In addition, these talks serve as an interesting introduction to a universal Sufism, with a wealth of Sufi stories and references to distinguished Sufi poets.

The power of creating a personality is an inner work with an outer effect. It is a practical means of coping with the excesses of our culture, the violence and despair we see around us, even among our children. Need I say that restoring belief in the human being is nothing short of an act of love in our time?

This group of lectures is edited from *The Complete Works of Pir-o-Murshid Hazrat Inayat Khan*, an on-going project, supported by the Nekbakht Foundation, which will, when finished, offer a complete chronological presentation of Inayat Khan's lectures. While Inayat Khan was giving the talks on creating the person in the summer of 1923, for example (first published as *Character Building. The Art of Personality*), he was also presenting a series on the soul, particularly on the soul's manifestation, which was edited early on into a volume entitled *The Soul: Whence and Whither?* These two series seem complementary: one emphasizing the scope of the individual, the other a cosmology of the soul. We see this same methodology in other series of lectures as well. In 1922, for example, a series entitled "The Problem of the Day" alternates with one entitled "The Inner Life."

iv

This method of emphasizing both ends of a polarity is, in fact, one of the methods of both the ancient and modern Sufis. In his *Bezels of Wisdom*, Ibn 'Arabi (1165-1240) describes the perfect man in this way: "He is at once ephemeral and eternal, a being created perpetual and immortal, a verb discriminating (by his distinctive knowledge) and unifying (by his divine essence)."[1] And Pir Vilayat Inayat Khan (b. 1916), in his numerous books and articles, utilizes this approach as well. To preserve the complementarity of Pir-o-Murshid Inayat Khan's method, a new volume on the material dealing with the soul is planned for the not too distant future.

The material presented here does not exhaust Inayat Khan's teachings on this subject of character and personality. Many relevant talks can be found, for example, in the *Gathas* (published as volume 13 of the *Sufi Message* series). In fact, pertinent material can be found in lectures throughout the summer of 1923, when, for instance, Inayat Khan was asked "Is the form of mind character?" He replied, "No, the soul, the spirit of man, is his character. The form of the mind is what the mind thinks about."

Two additional talks, published neither in the *Gathas* nor in the original or subsequent editions of the material presented here, have been included here for the first time: "Graciousness" and "Reconciliation." Indeed, this is the first time that "Reconciliation" has been published at all, apart from its appearance in *The Complete Works of Pir-o-Murshid Hazrat Inayat Khan: 1923:II*. The same is true for the questions and answers; these have never been published before, except in *The Complete Works*, and are included here, with the questions left more or less as they were asked.

A note on the editing: The reason that these numerous lectures have been so carefully preserved has to do with the care with which one of Pir-o-Murshid Inayat Khan's secretaries, Sakina Furnée, recorded them in shorthand. She took down the words exactly as Inayat Khan gave them in a Dutch shorthand system in a form specifically developed for recording the English language. In addition, the Pir-o-Murshid himself asked that his exact words be retained in publication. "Do not change my words, form, or phrase unless it is most necessary. Even so, most carefully avoid all changes which can be avoided." He felt that his speech and phrasing were as essential to his meaning as the perfume in the rose; he asked that his wording be preserved even if it did not seem as correct as it ought to be from a literary point of view. "Just now, if my words are not accepted as the current coin, they will always be valued as the antique."

Original and subsequent publications of this material have been extensively edited. In this volume, I have tried to preserve his actual words whenever possible. And, although in general I prefer a gender-inclusive text, I am experimenting with not blindly following my own principles in the interest of not over-editing the material. I have, however, included a sample of the first lecture edited according to gender-inclusive principles in the appendix. Please feel free to employ this technique in your reading of this material. Brackets in the text [ ] represent a missing word which has been supplied for context. Grammatical problems have been silently solved. I have also employed the current standard style of capitalization, in which only the name of God is capitalized and not pronouns or attributes.

J. Kore Salvato

# Acknowledgements

I would like to thank my Associate Editor on this project, Vakil Nancy Wilkinson, whose quiet enthusiasm and steady hand have helped bring this project to fruition. My editorial consultant Sharif Donald Graham, who is both the editor of *The Complete Works of Pir-o-Murshid Hazrat Inayat Khan* and my husband, offered insightful comments, willing help and a sense of humor--all of which were much appreciated. In addition, I would like to thank the late Munira van Voorst van Beest, the founding editor of *The Complete Works*, who initially suggested this project; Berthi van der Bent Hamel for her encouragement; and Abi'l-Khayr of Omega Publications. Kashfinur Heine provided technical support, and Fravarti Kim O'Haire proofread the final draft.

# I

# *Will Power*

Will power plays a great part in character building, and will power becomes feeble when a person yields to every little tendency, inclination, and fancy he has. When a person fights against every little fancy and tendency and inclination, one learns to fight with oneself, and in this way one develops will power. When once a person's inclinations, fancies, and tendencies have grown stronger than his will power, then one experiences in one's life several enemies existing in one's own self, and one finds it difficult to combat them; for inclinations, fancies and tendencies, when powerful, do not let will power work against them. If there is anything like self-denial, it is this practice; and by this practice, in time, one attains to a power which may be called mastery over one's self.

In small things of everyday life one neglects this consideration for the reason that one thinks "these are my tendencies, my fancies, my inclinations—and by respecting them I respect myself; by considering them I consider myself." But one forgets that what one calls "me" is not oneself. It is what wills that is oneself. Therefore, in the Christian prayer it is taught "Thy will be done," which means "Thy will, when it works through me, will be done"; in other words, "My will, which is thy will, will be done." It is this illusion of muddling one's possession with oneself that creates all illusion and keeps man from self-realization.

Life is a continual battle. Man struggles with things which are outside of him, and so he gives a chance to the

1

foes who exist in his own being.[2] Therefore, the first thing necessary in life is to make peace for the time being with the outside world in order to prepare for the war which is to be fought within oneself. Once peace is made within, one will gain by that sufficient strength and power to be used in the struggle of life within and without.

Self-pity is the worst poverty. When a person says "I am ..." with pity, before he has said anything more, he has diminished what he is to half, and what is said further diminishes him totally. Nothing more is left of him afterwards. There is so much in the world which we can pity and on which it would be right for us to take pity. But if we have no time free from our own self, we cannot give mind to the condition of others in the world. Life is one long journey, and the more we have left ourselves behind, the further we have progressed toward the goal. Verily, when the false self is lost, the true self is discovered.

\* \* \*

*Question: Why do we find satisfaction in self-pity?*
Answer: The reason is that by nature we find satisfaction in love. And when we are confined to ourselves, we begin to love ourselves; for our limitations we have self-pity. But, therefore, the love of self always brings dissatisfaction, because the self is made to love, and, when we love, the first condition of love is that we forget our self. We cannot love another person by loving our self at the same time. The condition of love is to forget oneself; then one knows how to love. If one says "Give me a sixpence and I will give you a shilling," that is another kind of love.

*Question: Do you mean by the false self, the ego?*
Answer: Yes, by the false self I mean false ego, the deluding ego, someone who has guised himself as the ego. The reason is that man's ego is false ego. What is ego? It is that

line which connects God and man; that line, one end of which is man, the other is God. Therefore, that end which is man's ego is false, because man has covered it with false ego. The ego is true. It is divine, it cannot be anything else. But man covers it with illusions and calls it "me," "myself." When that wrong conception is broken by knowledge, love, wisdom, or meditation, then it is just like the clouds which are broken, which cover the sun; and the true ego comes out, the only ego there is.

*Question: Is it easy to say "Thy will be done"?*
Answer: There are two ways of looking at it: the way of the master and of the saint. The way of the saint is "Thy will be done"; the way of the master is "My will be done." In the end both things become one. But to say "Thy will be done" is a resignation.

*Question: Is it possible for an ego to come on earth and never be covered by clouds of illusion?*
Answer: No, the beauty is to come out of that illusion. If one came wise, there would be no joy in coming out of it. The joy is in the unveiling.
　　　The question is, what is the ego? It is the ego in us which says "I." It is that ego which says, "This is mine." When a person says "I am sorry," what is it in him that says "I am sorry"? It is his ego, not his hand, his eye, his ear.

*Question: The difference between the false and real ego is the difference between selfishness and unselfishness?*
Answer: Yes, the result of the manifestation of the real ego is unselfishness. It is a natural outcome of it. And the more one is absorbed in the false ego, the more selfish that person is.

*Question: To say "I am sorry" is an act of compassion. How then can the false ego say this?*

Answer: The real ego does not know sorrow; it is happiness. We long for happiness because our true being is happiness. God is happiness. There are many people who do not long for God, but they long for happiness. It is the same thing. For instance, an atheist: he says there is no God, but he longs for happiness. God is happiness.

*Question: What really is the character?*
Answer: Character is, so to speak, a picture with lines and colors we make within ourselves. And it is wonderful to see how the tendency of character building springs up from childhood, just like one sees the instinct of building a nest in a bird. The little child begins to note everything in the grown-up people and begins to adopt all that seems to it the best: the word, the manner, the movement, the idea, everything that it grasps from the grown-up—whatever seems to its own mind best. It attracts it and it builds, so to speak, a building, which is its character. It is being built all through the life.

By this we understand that when a person is absorbed in the self, one has no time to see the other; then there is no other. But when one forgets oneself, one has the time to see here and there and add naturally to one's character. So the character is built. One need not make an effort in building the character if only one forgets oneself. For instance, if the great actors and actresses, with great qualifications, do not forget their selves, they cannot act; they may have all capability. So a musician, when he cannot forget at the time when he is playing, he cannot perform music to satisfaction. So with the poet, the artist. Think, then: the whole work of building oneself and everything else, it all depends upon how much one is able to forget oneself, which is the key to the whole life, material and spiritual life, and to success. It seems such a simple thing, and yet it is so difficult.

The wonderful thing is that during my travels,

whenever I have met very great people in anything—art, science, thought, religion, philosophy, whatever be their work—I have found that they have touched that greatness with this quality, the quality of forgetting themselves. Always, everywhere it is the same.

And I have again seen people with great qualifications, but they remember themselves so much that they cannot do the best with their lives. I have known a vina player who tried so much, playing his instrument for six, nine hours a day. But whenever he used to go in the assembly, he became so nervous because he thought of himself. And all the impressions of the people would fall upon him. He would take his instrument and cover it and run away. He never had a chance of being great, even with all his qualifications.

Self-confidence is a great thing, but forgetting oneself is greater still.

I have seen Sarah Bernhardt. She was singing a very simple song, the National Anthem of France. When she came on the stage she won every person there. At that time she was the nation; with that sentiment in the feeling and the words, she was France at that time, because of her concentration.

## II

# *The Music of Life*

In character building it is most necessary that one learn how to face the world, the world where one meets with sorrows and troubles and pleasures and pains. It is very difficult for one to hide from the world, and at the same time a wise person is not meant to show all he feels at every moment. An ordinary person, like a machine, reacts in answer to every outer influence and inner impulse, and in this way very often cannot keep to the law of the music of life.

Life, to a wise person, is a music, and in that symphony he has to play a certain part. If, in one's feeling, one has dropped down so low that one's heart is sounding a lower pitch, and the demand of life at that moment is that one must voice a higher pitch, at that time one finds that one has failed that music in which one was meant to play his part fittingly.

This is the test by which you can distinguish the old soul and the child soul. The child soul will give a way to every feeling; the old soul will strike the higher note in spite of all difficulties. There are moments when laughter must be kept back, and there are times when tears must be withdrawn. And those who have arrived at the stage where they can act the part that they are meant to act in this life's drama rightly and efficiently, they even have power over the expression on their face. They can even turn their tears into smiles, or smiles into tears. One may ask: "Is it not hypocrisy not to be natural?" The one who has control over his nature is more natural. He is not only natural, but he is the master of nature. The one who lacks power over nature, in spite of his naturalness, is weak.

Besides, it must be understood that real civilization means the art of life. What is that art? It is the knowing of the music of life. Once a soul has awakened to the continual music of life, the soul will consider as its responsibility, as its duty, to play its part in the outer life, even if it be contrary to its inner condition for the moment. To do this, it requires knowledge.

One must know at every moment in one's daily life, "What does life demand of me, what does it ask of me, and how shall I answer the demand of my life?" This requires one to be awakened fully to life's conditions. One must have insight into human nature, and one must be able to know one's own condition fully as well. If one says, "I am as I am; if I am sad, I am sad, if I am glad, I am glad," that will not do. Even the earth will not bear that person who will not answer life's demands. The sky will not tolerate that person, and the space will not accommodate him who is not ready to give what life asks of him. If this is true, then it is best when it is wisely done, and willingly done.

In the orchestra there is a conductor and there are many who play music, and every player of an instrument has to fill in his contribution in the performance. If he does not do it right, it is his fault. The conductor will not listen that he did not do it right because he was sad, or that he was too glad; the conductor is not concerned with his sadness or gladness. He is concerned with the part that the particular musician must play in the whole symphony. That is the nature of our lives. The further we advance, our part in this orchestra becomes more difficult and more important, and the more conscious we become of this responsibility, the more efficient we become in performing our part in life's symphony satisfactorily.

In order to be able to have that control over oneself,

what is necessary? We must have control over our inner self, because every outward manifestation is nothing but a reaction of the inner condition. Therefore, the first control that we have to get is over ourselves, our inner self, which is done by strengthening the will, and by understanding life better.

* * *

*Question: Are the beings who live on the other planets humans or angels?*
Answer: On any part of the earth human beings live. Our planet is the earth. No doubt there are differences in the evolution of the people living on different planets. Yet on all planets there are angelic people and those who are the contrary.

*Question: How do the earth and the sky and space not bear and accommodate the person who does not answer life's demands?*
Answer: Have you, perhaps, heard of a person who has been exiled from, perhaps, five different countries, and perhaps went to a sixth, and was also exiled? The earth cannot bear him. They would like to put him in the water, to burn him, because the earth does not want him to walk upon her. It is what is called the curse. The curse manifests in many forms. A person takes that with him. He may go from the south pole to the north pole; when the earth once does not want him, it does not want him wherever he goes. Among the primitive people they will want to eat him because the earth cannot bear him.

With exceptional souls there is an exceptional law. It cannot be explained with ordinary terms of expression. Great souls also go from one place to another; it is not that the earth does not bear them, but human beings.

*Question: What will be the future of those who have not*

*fulfiled the demand of life? Shall they come back to learn the lesson again?*

Answer: We must all learn our lesson just now. They may come back or not come back—that is another question. Just now the question is before us; life's demand is just now, not after life. At every moment of our life we are asked to fulfil a certain duty, a certain work, in everything we do. With every movement we are fulfilling a certain duty, consciously or unconsciously. To become conscious of it, and do it fittingly and rightly, that is the true religion.

*Question: What do you mean by older and younger souls?*

Answer: In this particular case I only meant ripened and unripened souls. The older soul is just like an older brother, the younger like a younger brother.

*Question: The last sentence [of your lecture] was, ". . .also by understanding life better." What is the wisest way to understand?*

Answer: In this last sentence I meant that we understand life's demands by understanding life better. And if we do not understand life better, we cannot understand fully what life asks of us. There are some who do not answer life's demands because they do not know what life asks of them. There are others who know what life asks of them, but they have not yet advanced enough to do it. In order to know what life asks, one must understand life better.

*Question: One may ask, perhaps, "When what our outer life demands is quite different from what the inner life asks of us, which do we listen to?"*

Answer: In the Bible there is a beautiful answer to this question: "Give unto Caesar what Caesar asks, and to God what God asks." What the outer life demands, those demands must be fulfiled, and what the inner life demands, we must also fulfil.

A murshid was travelling with three or four mureeds during that season in the East when people have their fastings for so many days—every day they fast.[3] This murshid was visiting in a village, at a peasant's house. The peasant was so happy that the murshid had come with his pupils that there was no end of joy. He went to the market and bought all the good things he could get and prepared a lunch, without asking the murshid or the pupils. And the lunch was brought to the table.

According to the religious law, and also the spiritual law, it is a very bad thing to break the law of fasting. It is a sacred law, a religious law. So every mureed[4] refused. This peasant could not understand why they refused. They were too modest to say that they were fasting, but at the same time they did not break their vows. When he came to the murshid, the murshid said, "Yes," and very gladly sat at the table with the family. The peasant was very pleased, and very sorry that all these young men did not eat. They thought, "Our murshid has perhaps forgotten; he is perhaps in his dreams."

After the dinner was finished, the peasant was very glad. When they went out, one of the daring pupils came to the murshid: "Murshid, I am sorry to say, perhaps you have forgotten that we are fasting." He said, "No, child, I have not forgotten; I would rather break the fast, however sacred, than to break the heart of the one who prepared that food for me." That was the idea. It is to answer life's demands. At that time life had demanded that the murshid keep his word, though inwardly.

*Question: When one may not hold tight to any original plane and gets into all sorts of unhappy circumstances, how to get out of this best?*
Answer: We do not need to waken ourselves to any particular plane. For we shall waken to every plane as we go on in life's journey. What is necessary is to be wide

awake through life and see what is asked of us by our friend, by our neighbor, by our acquaintance, by a stranger who is travelling with us.

It is just becoming more and more considerate, and observing more clearly what another expects of us. Do we harm him, or do we serve him; are we kind to that person, or are we cruel? Because everyone through life has his motive before him, and in going toward that motive he is often apt to forget whom he pushes away, and whom he hurts, and on whom he treads, and to whom he becomes unjust, and to whom he becomes unkind. The one who does not observe makes perhaps a hundred mistakes. It does not mean that one can be without mistakes. Still, if one can avoid nine hundred out of a thousand, it is something.

*Question: The greatest difficulty seems to me not to accord with the sad and the joyful, but to go together with those who go in another direction and who will other things. What does wisdom teach in this direction, in order not to fight with them and still to go your own direction?*

Answer: To go in your own direction is good as long as you understand your own direction and your own [willingness]. Nothing, however good it appears, is a virtue unless it is willingly done, because in the willingness in doing a sacrifice, there one experiences the breath of freedom. A virtue which is forced upon oneself or another is not a virtue; it loses its beauty. We must do what seems good to us. If we think that it is a virtue to keep to our own idea, or if we think that giving up our idea to follow the idea of another is a virtue, then it is a virtue when there is willingness. Virtue must not be forced.

# III

# *Self-Control*

In everyday life, what is most necessary is to have control of speech and action, for one automatically gives a way to a word prompted by an inner impulse. Afterwards, one finds that one should not have said it, or perhaps one would have said it differently. It is the same thing with action. One feels "I should not have done so" after having done something, or one thinks "I should have done differently"; but once it is done, it is too late to do it otherwise.

In human nature there is an inner urge to express oneself, and that urge, so to speak, pushes a word out of oneself before one has thought it over. And this all shows the sign of a lack of control over oneself. It also is a sign of nervousness. Very often a person tries to answer somebody who has not yet finished speaking; before a sentence is completed the answer is given. Such an answer given to an incomplete idea is often not right. What generally happens in such cases is that one takes all things in life that come from outside too much to heart and allows the outer things and influences to go into oneself deeper than they are due. In this way one becomes sensitive, and out of it rises nervousness.

In order to practice self-control in everything one does in everyday life, the best thing is to develop in one's nature a certain amount of indifference. Every word that is said to one need not be taken to be so important that it should upset one's whole being, disturb one's balance, and rob one of one's will power. There are things that matter, but there are many things in one's everyday life which do not matter much and one often is apt to put an undue stress upon them. Independence is achieved by indifference. It does not mean that one should take no heed of what another does or says. It only means to discriminate between important and unimportant things of everyday life, that every necessary and unnecessary thing must not demand so much of one's attention, thought, and feeling.

Political economy has become a subject of education, but spiritual economy is the main thing in religion. All one says and does and all that one thinks and feels makes a certain strain upon one's spirit. It is wise to avoid every chance of losing one's equilibrium. One must stand peacefully but firmly against all influences that disturb one's life.

The natural inclination is to answer in defence every offence that comes from outside; by that, one loses one's equilibrium. Self-control, therefore, is the key to all success and happiness. Besides this, there are many who feel urged and obliged to say or do because someone asks of them, and in this way they get weaker and weaker; there are others who roughly fight against it, and in this way both are in error. The one who is able to keep his equilibrium without being annoyed, without being troubled about it, gains that mastery which is needed in the evolution of life.

No principle must be blindly followed. Spiritual economy is not always a virtue if it disturbs harmony, if it in any way keeps one back from progressing, if it puts one in a worse condition. However, it is most necessary to know the science of spiritual economy, how to guard against all influences in one's everyday life which come to disturb our tranquillity, the peace of our soul.

* * *

*Question: What is the meaning of the symbol of the fish?*
Answer: The symbol of the fish is the sign of the heart. And as the fish out of water finds itself out of place and experiences discomfort, so the heart when it is not living and moving and making its life in love feels out of place, and all discomfort of life comes from it.

*Question: Please explain the belief that one is taught in the Church, that Christ died to save us.*
Answer: Yes, apart from those who do not follow the Christian faith, there are many even who are Christian who question whether there is some truth in this. And yet it is so simple to understand that the soul of the God-conscious truly lived and moved and made his life in God. His every word, every thought, and every action was directed to the service of humanity, and he kept nothing back from sacrificing for humanity, even his life. And therefore, no appreciative heart who looked at this question in this way would ever deny the fact that Christ gave his life to save humanity. This can be the best expression of that appreciation which one can have of that self-sacrificing soul who proved, through his life, divinity.

*Question: What does the soul do at night when the body sleeps?*
Answer: Poor soul, upon the poor soul there are so many demands. When the body is awake, then it must wander with the body, wherever it will take it. When the body is asleep it must go with the mind; where the mind takes it, it goes. Of course in this connection one must think of that sentence in the Bible, "Where your treasure is, there your heart will be also." It is not the heart, it is soul there where the treasure is. Is it in heaven? Then it is in heaven. Is it on earth? Then it is on earth. If the treasure is in the purse, then the soul is in the purse; if it is in music, poetry,

14

philosophy, or thought, then the soul is with that. All one admires, values, loves in life, the soul is with it. If one loves sadness, then the soul is in sadness; if one loves to experience joy, then the soul is joyous. What one seeks after, that is where the soul goes.

Yet the soul touches all spheres from the lowest to the highest. Even the soul of the most wicked person touches all spheres, only he does not experience the benefit of it, because when he is conscious he is tasting wickedness. But when the soul is unconscious and touches the highest, what is the use? Therefore, as it is mentioned in *The Message of Spiritual Liberty*,[5] there are many paths, even ones that one could never imagine—one would be horrified if one knew the different ways—by which a person could arrive at the same goal. Still the thing is this, that the blessing of life is in the consciousness of that blessing. When one is not conscious of that blessing, it is nothing. If a kitten is privileged to sit on the sofa of the king and is dwelling all the time at Buckingham Palace, it is not privileged when it is not conscious of the privilege.

*Question: Would you tell us how far it is right to take the individual temper into account in trying to build character?*
Answer: I personally, if I were to advise myself, would take extreme measures in keeping individuality pliable, not set to a certain temper. No doubt individuality is made of a certain temper, but I would not personally allow it to set to a certain temper. For another person, I would not advise an extreme measure.

I will tell you an experience of my own life. Once I began my musical work and, having that sensitiveness of an artist, if there was among my audience of five, ten, twenty people, one person lacking understanding or antagonistic to it, it would choke my breast and I would not be able to do anything. I saw it one, two, three times; but how could I do my work? The next day I said, "I shall shake it off, not take it into account. I shall sing for myself; if no one shall enjoy it, I shall still sing. If I am pleased, it is quite enough."Since that feeling came, that artistic temper went to pieces. It never came again. That is fighting against temper.

What is temper? It is a nature we make. What makes a nature? We have something of it; in making it, we enjoy it. By saying, "I hate it, I cannot stand, tolerate it," one does not know what he is doing. One has confined himself to a limitation, a weakness. Why can I not tolerate? Then I cannot tolerate myself. I cannot bear it. There will come a day when one cannot bear oneself.

It is a terrible fight because the self begins to cry for nights and days. The self says, "You are my worst enemy in the world, you are so cruel, you have no pity on me," because it feels crushed. But when it is once crushed and has come under the control of will power, then one begins to feel that the Kingdom of God begins to come. Sometimes one feels that it is unjust, unfair, too cruel to oneself, and the difficulty is that the neighbors also say that you are too cruel to yourself. No one wants to encourage you in that direction.

*Question: Ascetic temperament . . .?*
Answer: One must not go against one's happiness, but there are some ascetic temperaments who fight with themselves. There is a great gain in it, because there are not many who do it. One must not even make principles so set that one cannot bear them. There are people who are born fighters, and their fight is with themselves.

*Question: There is a person who is a born fighter and his fight is with his self?*
Answer: There is a story of spiritual pride. Once a dervish was sitting in the wilderness on a rock in a comfortable position. Akbar, the emperor of Delhi, went to pay his

homage to this dervish. The dervish saw that the emperor had come and his minister was also there with him. But the dervish did not change his position. Of course Akbar did not feel uncomfortable about it. But the one who went with Akbar, he did not see from the point of view of the emperor. He felt that when he has to bow a thousand times to the king, why not this man? He asked him in a very polite way, "How long is it since you have stretched these legs?" He wanted to turn it into a kind of vow. The dervish answered, "Since I have withdrawn my hands. When the hands were the hands of greed, since I was in want, I had taken all I wanted of the world. There is nothing I want now; now my legs are stretched. If the emperor comes, it is all the same to me." That is a spiritual pride. But spiritual pride is a very delicate thing to understand. The pride that says, "I am so spiritual" has nothing spiritual about it. It is personal pride, because where there is spirituality, there is no "I am."

# IV

# *Relationship*

It is a most important thing in character building to become conscious of one's relation, obligation, and duty to each person in the world, and not to mix that link and connection which is established between oneself and another with a third person. One must think of everything that is entrusted to one by every person in life as one's trust, and one must know that to prove true to the confidence of every person in the world is one's sacred obligation. In this manner a harmonious connection is established with every person, and it is the harmony established with every person which tunes the soul with the infinite.

It requires a great study of human nature, together with tact, to keep on harmonious terms with every person in life. If one has admiration for someone or a grudge against someone, it is better to express it directly instead of mixing it up with many connections and relations in the world. Friendship apart, even with an acquaintance this consideration is necessary: to guard carefully that thin thread that connects two souls in whatever relation or capacity. *Dharma* in the language of the Hindus means religion, but the literal meaning of this word is duty. It suggests that one's relation to every person in the world is one's religion, and the more conscientiously one follows it, the more keen he proves in following his religion.

To keep the secret of our friend, our acquaintance, even of someone with whom for a time being one has been vexed, is the most sacred obligation. The one who thus realizes his religion, would he ever consider it right to tell another of any harm or hurt he has received from his friend? Never. It is in this that self-denial is learned, not always by fasting and retirement in the wilderness. The man who is conscientious of his duty, of his obligations to his friends, is more pious than someone sitting alone in solitude. The one in solitude does not serve God; he only helps himself by enjoying the pleasure of solitude. But the one who proves to be trustworthy to every soul he meets and considers his relation and connection, small or great, as something sacred, certainly observes the spiritual law of that religion which is the religion of religions.

Faults: everyone has faults. Oneself, one's friend, and one's enemy, all are subject to faults. The one who wishes that his own faults may not be disclosed must necessarily consider the same for the others he meets. If one only knew what the relation of friendship is between one soul and another, the tenderness of this connection, its delicacy, its beauty, and its sacredness, he could enjoy life in its fullness, for he would be living, and in this manner he must someday communicate with God. It is the same bridge which connects two souls in the world which, when once stretched, becomes the path to God. There is no greater virtue in this world than proving kind and trustworthy to one's friend, worthy of his confidence.

The difference between the old soul and the young soul is to be found in this particular principle. The young soul only knows himself and what he wants, absorbed in his own pleasures and displeasures and obsessed by his ever-changing moods. The old soul regards his relation to every soul; he keenly observes his obligations toward everyone he knows in the world. He covers his wounds, if he happens to have them, from the sight of the others and endures all things in order to fulfil his duty as best he can toward everyone in the world.

There is a story in the *Arabian Nights* which in some

way is incomprehensible, yet which explains in an exaggerated form the subject on which I have been speaking. Once a king was on a tour in the woods. Where he was camping there lived some robbers. A robber happened to go into the tent where the king was asleep and tried to get a ring from under his pillow. And when he was taking away that ring, the king got up and he looked at the thief and said, "Who are you?" He said, "I am a robber." "Why have you come here?" "To find if I can get something from you." "What did you find?" "I found your ring; here it is, shall I give it back to you?" The king said, "No, take it." The robber said, "Then do not tell anyone." "Certainly not," said the king.

\* \* \*

*Question: Can you please tell us why there is a legend in the* Talmud *that says Moses died from the kiss of God?*
Answer: I should say that anyone should die of the kiss of God. In the *Gayan*[6] is said, "'Sundew, why is it that every insect that kisses you dies instantly?' 'I love him so that I eat him up.'" The explanation is the same.

The condition of God and his true lover is only one, and that is, either the beloved lives or the lover. Therefore, Rumi says, "The Beloved is all in all, the lover only veils Him; love is all that lives, the lover a dead thing."

*Question: What must we do if others do not consider our friendship and do not wish to regard our views in life? Must we always go on to see them and try to come into contact with them if we are in some way related to them?*
Answer: I would never say to anybody, "Go and consider the friend who has ill-treated you," but, "Do what you consider best." There cannot be one principle for all to follow; for each there is a particular principle. But by considering the main principles of character building, then

20

one will be helped. It does not mean that one should follow exactly these principles which are spoken of as character building. But by knowing them, they can be a great help in choosing the best way in dealing with life. For the one who observes this principle certainly is on the saintly path, because such a principle requires a great sacrifice, renunciation, a great deal of self-denial. It wants an unselfish person who could follow this.

*Question: You spoke of covering the faults of others, but even of our own?*
Answer: Yes, this is a still higher form.

*Question: Can life be symbolized as a ladder?*
Answer: Yes.

*Question: Was it the ladder that Jacob saw?*
Answer: Yes, life's evolution is as a ladder. Every person is on a different step.

*Question: How is it to be understood that both Jesus and Buddha broke off all relations of friends and of their parents and came back from solitude as a stranger? Buddha especially says that no one can attain Nirvana who still has human relations.*
Answer: Yes, but this question is a question of renunciation. The question of character building is a different question. Life is like a ladder. The principle of one step is not the principle of another. On each step there is a particular principle. At the same time those who have risen above all relations, they observe the law of relationship more than anybody else. They become so conscious of their obligation, not only to their relations, but to every little insect and germ. Their relationship is only wider and stronger.
      The idea is that the claim of relationship is one

thing, and the observing of relationship with all is another stage. They have passed that stage of character building; they are above it, they cannot be compared.

# V

# *Subtlety*

Subtlety of nature is the sign of the intelligent. If a person takes the right direction, he does good with this wealth of intelligence. A person who is going in a wrong direction may abuse this great faculty. When a person who is subtle by nature is compared to a personality which is void of subtlety, it is like the river and the mountain. The subtle personality is as pliable as the running water; everything that comes before that personality is reflected in it as clearly as an image in pure water. The rock-like personality, void of subtlety, is like a mountain; it reflects nothing.

Many admire plain speaking, but the reason is their lack of understanding of fine subtlety. Can all things be put into words? Is there not anything more fine, more subtle than spoken words? The person who can read between the lines makes a book out of one letter. Subtlety of perception and subtlety of expression are the signs of the wise.

Wise and foolish are distinguished by fineness on the part of the one, and rigidness on the part of the other. A person void of subtlety wants truth to be turned into a stone, and the subtle one will even turn a stone into truth. In order to acquire spiritual knowledge, in order to receive inspiration, in order to prepare one's heart for inner revelation, one must try and make one's mentality pliable like water, rather than like a rock. For the further in the path of life's mystery a person will sojourn, the more subtle he will have to become in order to perceive and to express the mystery of life. God is a mystery; his knowledge is a mystery. Life is a mystery; human nature is a mystery. In short, the depth of all knowledge is a mystery. Even in science or art, all that is more mysterious is deeper.

What all the prophets and masters have done in all ages is to express that mystery in words, in deeds, in thoughts, in feelings. But most of the mystery is expressed by them in silence, for then the mystery is in its place. To bring down the mystery to the ground is like pulling down a king on to the ground from his throne. But allowing the mystery to remain in its own place, in the silent spheres, is like giving homage to the king to whom all homage is due.

Life's mysteries apart, in little things of everyday life the less words used the more profitable it is. Do you think more words explain more? No, not at all. It is only nervousness on the part of those who wish to say a hundred words to explain a thing which can quite well be explained in two words. And on the part of the listener it is a lack of intelligence when he wants a hundred words in order to understand something which can just as well be explained in one word. Many think that more words explain things better, but they do not know that most often the more words spoken, so many more veils are wrapped around the idea. In the end you go out by the same door by which you have entered.

Respect, consideration, reverence, kindness, compassion and sympathy, forgiveness and gratefulness: all these virtues can be best adorned by subtlety of expression. One need not dance in thanksgiving; one word of thanks is quite sufficient. One need not play drums that "I have forgiven somebody." One need not cry out loud that "I sympathize with you, my dear friend." Such things are fine, subtle; they are to be felt. No noise can express them; noise only spoils their beauty and takes from their value.

In spiritual ideas and thoughts subtlety is more needed than in anything else. If a spiritual person were to bring his realizations to the marketplace and dispute with everyone that came along about his beliefs and disbeliefs, where would he end?

What makes a spiritual person harmonize with all people in the world? The key to the art of reconciliation that a spiritual soul has is subtlety in both perception and expression. Is it lack of frankness? Is it hypocrisy to be subtle? Not in the least. There are many people who are outspoken, as ready to tell the truth as to hit the head of another person. They proudly support their frankness by saying, "I do not mind if it makes anybody sorry or angry. I only tell the truth." If the truth is as hard as a hammer, may truth never be spoken! May no one in the world follow such truth!

Then what is that truth which is peace-giving, which is healing, which is comforting to every heart and soul? That truth which uplifts the soul, that truth which is creative of harmony and beauty—where is that truth born? That truth is born in subtlety of intelligence, of thought, speech, and action; in fineness, which brings pleasure, comfort, beauty, harmony, and peace.

\* \* \*

*Question: Will you explain that the heart of man is the heart of the universe?*
Answer: In the heart of man the whole universe is reflected, and as the whole universe is reflected in the heart of man, it may be called the heart of the universe.

*Question: What is the heart and what is the soul?*
Answer: Suppose we take a lamp, a burning lamp, as a picture of the human being. The flame is the soul, and the globe is the heart. The inner part of the globe is called the heart, the outer part is the mind, and the shade over the lamp is the body.

*Question: Will you explain the difference between a child soul and a grown-up soul?*

Answer: The difference is that of a ripe fruit and an unripened fruit. It is just like a grown-up man who has more experience compared with the child, and by his experience he has learned and understood more. So is a soul who may be a young person and yet he may have a greater understanding because of his soul being ripe.

*Question: How can one cultivate this subtleness; I thought one was born with it, and could not acquire it?*

Answer: If one knew how wonderful is the life of man, of whom God says that "I have created man in my own image." Is there anything which is not in God? If all things are in God, then all things are in man, whom he has made in his own image. No doubt, the things that he tries to acquire he is able to acquire them better; the things that he neglects, he does not . . . .

Often we see people with intelligence, with a brain, yet who are unwilling to trouble their brain very much, for they do not want to trouble; it is not that they cannot understand. If they can get it easily explained by someone, they do not want to trouble. Very often one sees that. And therefore, subtlety is a fineness. Such fineness can be acquired by the love of fineness, not only in human character, but in everything.

If an artist has not the love of subtlety, his art will only be on the surface. It will become living if he has subtlety in his nature. So with poetry. If the poet only writes words, nothing behind it, that does not give life, that is only the structure. What makes a verse beautiful? Twist. A person could write five lines and make the soul dance at its fineness, its subtlety. Another person will write a hundred letters, and it means nothing: too many words, tiredness is the only result of it. The book of Rumi[7] has lived hundreds of years; the interest is always growing.

26

Why? Because there is subtlety from the beginning to the end.

When one does not take the trouble to cultivate fineness in nature and subtlety in perception and expression, it is just like a stubborn child who wants his food to be put in his mouth. He does not want to take the trouble of eating himself. A subtle person is only a conscientious person, a person on his guard, who has taken life as a horse: he has the rein in his hand; he makes it dance when he wants it to dance, lets it go slowly when he wants. A dancer, a poet, a singer—in every aspect, in all one does, subtlety produces beauty. Subtlety is the curl of the beloved, a symbolical expression used by Omar Khayyam and most of the Sufi poets.[8]

*Question: How is the periodic coming and going of events, cataclysms, wars, etc., to be explained, as well as the fact of the possibility of a purely mathematical reading of all life in astrology? These things seem to speak in favor of the idea that all life is an automatically running clock, and that there is no liberty of action and thought. (Death of a babe or child.) What is the sense of a human being dying before it has reached a certain development? It seems a great waste of energy, and a great suffering in vain.*

Answer: The first question, in which it is asked if the whole universe is going on automatically and there is no free will, the answer is that, yes, a man is born in a universe which is going on automatically, and he is born helpless. Therefore, it is true that the condition is such. But what is the child born with? He is born with a desire to do as he wills. This desire is the proof of there being a free will, a free will which is put to test under all opposing conditions and influences which the soul meets with through life. And to rise above all the opposing influences and to give the fullest expression to the free will brings about that result of life which is the fulfilment of the soul's coming on earth.

The second question: the reason for many things having sprung out of this automatically working universe, such as the birth of a babe who has passed soon after, and one does not see the reason behind it. But in this case we must understand that although outwardly it is automatically working, inwardly there is God. There is no mechanism without an engineer. Only the engineer does not seem to be standing by the side of the machine. And he is not claiming that he is the engineer. One thinks that there is a machine going on and there is no engineer. If one knew that there is an engineer, what can a little part of the machine understand about the scheme and plan which is made for the working of the whole universe? And if anybody understands, it is the awakened soul, but how much does he understand? Very little does he understand. And how does he, and what? He can only say what he can about it. That all justice or injustice, however it may seem to us on the surface, will all fit in and be perfect at the finish when there is the summing up of the working of the whole universe. There is a saying in support of this in the *Vadan*.[9]

# VI

# *Complaining and Smiling*

There are two attitudes which divide people into sections. The one attitude is an ever-complaining attitude, and the other attitude is an ever-smiling attitude. Life is the same; call it good, call it bad, call it right or call it wrong. It is what it is; it cannot be otherwise.

A person complains in order to get the sympathy of others, in order to show his good points to others, and sometimes in order to show himself more just, more intelligent and in the right. He complains about everything, about friends and about foes, about those he loves and much more so about those he hates. He complains from morning till evening, and there is never an end to his complaint. It can increase to such an extent that the weather is not good, and the air is not good, and the atmosphere is not good. He is against earth and sky both.

Everything everybody does is wrong until it develops to such a stage that man begins to dislike his own words, and it culminates when he dislikes himself. In this way one becomes against others, against conditions, and in the end against himself.

Do not imagine that this is a character rarely to be found in the world; it is a character with whom you frequently meet. And certainly the one who has this attitude is his worst enemy. The person with a right attitude of mind tries to make even wrong into right, but the one with a wrong attitude of mind will turn even right into wrong.

Besides, magnetism is something which is the need of every soul. The lack of it makes life burdensome. The tendency of seeing wrong in everything robs one greatly of that magnetism which is needed very much in life. For the nature of life is such that, by nature, the life of the multitude throws out everyone and accepts only those who enter the multitude with the power of magnetism. In other words, the world is a place where you cannot enter without a pass of admission, and that pass of admission is magnetism. The one who does not possess it will be refused everywhere.

Besides, you will find many who complain always about their health. There may be a reason, and sometimes there may be a very little reason, too little indeed to speak of. And when once a person has become accustomed to answer in the negative, when sympathetically asked, "How are you?", he certainly waters the plant of illness in himself by the complaining tendency.

Our life of limitation in the world and the nature of this world's comforts and pleasures, which are so changeable and unreliable, and the falsehood that one finds in everything, everywhere—if one complained about it all, a lifetime would be too short to complain about it fully. Every moment of our life would become filled with complaints. But the way out of it is to look at the cheerful side of it, the bright side of it. Especially those who seek God and truth, for them there is something else to think about. They need not think how bad the person is; when they think who is behind this person, who is in the heart of this person, then they will look at life with hope. When we see things wrong, if we only think that behind all workings there is God, who is just and perfect, then we certainly will become hopeful.

The attitude of looking at everything with a smile is the sign of the saintly soul. A smile given to a friend, a smile given even to an enemy will win him over in the end, for that is the key to the heart of man. As the sunshine from without lights the whole world, so the sunshine from within, if it were raised, would illuminate the whole life, in spite of all the seeming wrongs and in spite of all limitations. God is happiness, the soul is happiness, spirituality is happiness. There is no place for sadness in the kingdom of God. That which deprives man of happiness, deprives him of God and of truth.

One can begin to learn to smile by appreciating every little good thing that comes one's way through life, and by overlooking every bad thing that one does not like to see; by not troubling too much about unnecessary things in life which give nothing but displeasure, and by looking at life with a hopeful attitude of mind, with an optimistic view. It is this which will give one the power of turning wrong into right, and bringing light in the place where all is darkness. Cheerfulness is life; sulkiness is death. Life attracts; death repulses. The sunshine which comes from the soul, rises through the heart, and manifests in man's smile is indeed the light from the heavens. In that light many flowers grow, and many fruits become ripe.

\* \* \*

*Question: "Thou shalt not kill," and "Love thy neighbor as thyself," are written in the Bible. Has then the state the right to condemn someone to death?*
Answer: This was not said to the state, it was said to the individual. The law is not the same. The state is responsible for many individuals; therefore, its rights and laws are different. Suppose it had been possible in the Christian countries to obey this law, there would not have been war or any kind of killing. And suppose that the government allowed it when anybody killed a thief or robber, and the state said, "We are told not to kill." What would happen? The killing would increase; it would always increase.

Besides that, human nature is such that it comes from animal nature; every man does not live by the law of a scripture. Every man is born selfish; every man wants to get all he wants, even at the sacrifice of the life of another. If the revolver or sword were not used at all, it would be a beautiful thing, but what would happen? Should all human beings think as a saint thinks? The law given by Christ to his disciples was given to those who were seeking God and truth. Is it everybody who is trying to find God and truth? Everybody is living for the struggle of life. Therefore, in all cases the law that is given for an individual is not applicable for all, although one cannot deny the beauty of the teaching, which will certainly help those who take the path of truth in the search of love and kindness.

But then I will tell you another thing. In one place it is said, "Thou shalt not kill." In another place Christ said to unsheathe the sword.[10] If the sword were not for any use, or were to be condemned, there would not have been that suggestion. But besides this, I ask: if the religion of Christ has existed throughout the world, can one take away credit from the sword? If it had not been for the sword, the religion of Christ would not have spread. The blood of the martyrs is the foundation of the Church, those who have exposed themselves for the cause, for the message. Without them the world would not have known the message of Christ; few would have known it, and it would have been extinguished. It was meant that it should be.

The sword has its place in bringing the message of the master, not only in the life and mission of Christ, but in the mission of the great Hindu teachers, Rama and Krishna. Moses, who was before Christ, had to take the sword. Therefore, the sword is something which today we do not need so much for religion, but it could not have been condemned at the time when it was necessary. Even today, if all the nations decided that there should be no arms, the police would have to have swords just the same. The condition of the world and human nature will not allow for the world to exist without a sword at the present time. We must hope that in the future man may evolve, that there will be no necessity for the sword. But now it cannot be practical.

Psychology must not be forgotten when discussing moral principles. Moral principles teach us that we should be kind, forgiving, we should even give our life, if it were asked, for love, truth, or kindness. But would that mean that we should go before a lion and say, "Here my life is, a prey for you; please come and eat me." For the lion will never understand the principle, he will only be too glad to eat you.

There are human beings worse than the lion. Even the lion will understand the moral principle, but not man; and many men are like this. What will you do with them? They will take your life and all that you have besides. The lion will leave the bones, but the human being will not. He will even use the skin, every bit of one. Balance is the great thing: to understand morals and to understand psychology. When there is a divergence between these two things, then religion becomes unbalanced. Religion is not only for saints. Saints do not need it. Religion must have a balance, which is sent as the Message from time to time in order to give that same religion which is given before all men, to understand what is right for them and what is truly asked of them by God.

*Question: When a person with a cheerful attitude lives with a person with a sulky attitude of mind, and sees that his own cheerfulness even irritates the other, what can he do; is tact the only thing?*

Answer: You see, sulkiness is the attribute of a child soul. The sad soul is not a grown-up soul. Treat the child soul like a child. Do not take it to heart, do not take it too seriously. Even the tears of such a person, take them as flowers dropping from the plant. A child cries easily, also such a person. Only lift that person up for that time. But when you will try to sympathize, you will produce more gloom. Never sympathize at that time. Only say, "It is nothing."

There is something else: just to lift that person's consciousness. It is a kind of net in which the consciousness is caught. Lift it up. It is just like a bird, caught. Lift it out of that net. Do not let your own mind be impressed. If you allow it, then you have taken the germ of the disease; then gradually and slowly that disease will grow in you. The way of fighting against it is always to deny such a thing as sadness or depression in yourself and in another.

*Question: Why does the peasant say that one must sow the seed while the moon is growing, and not when it is waning? Has the moon really any influence, and why?*

Answer: Sufis also say, as the peasants say, "Do every new enterprise in life when there is a new moon, not in the waning moon." Because in that way you are in harmony with nature. In the new moon nature is progressive; in the waning moon, declining. The new moon is the day of nature, the waning moon is the night. Work during the day, rest during the night.

*Question: Can you give us the signification of this part of the Christ-prayer, "Lead us not into temptation"? Does God ever lead into temptation?*

Answer: It is only a matter of interpretation. You can quite see that the words of the Lord were given three hundred years before, and then brought to St Paul.[11] And then there were different versions and interpretations in different languages. All these things we must take into consideration. If I were to give an interpretation of this, I should say, "Let us not be led into temptation."

*Question: How must we explain, "Forgive us our trespasses as we forgive those who have trespassed against us"? And if we do not forgive?*

Answer: This is a suggestion; "Forgive us our trespasses as we forgive those" only means that "we are trying to forgive others for their trespasses, and so we expect that you will forgive us also." It does not mean that we have done it. It only means that we are trying to do it. We must remember that we cannot expect the forgiveness of God if forgiveness has not been awakened in our heart. The psychology is that the forgiveness of God is attracted by the spirit of forgiveness awakened in our heart. For instance, the relation between God and man apart, if a person who has practiced forgiveness in his life happens to do something wrong, you will feel ready to forgive him—because of what he has practiced you will gladly do the same to him. With another person who has not practiced this, with all your desire, you will feel a kind of difficulty, because this person does not help to make it easy for you to forgive. Does it not explain that we help God to forgive us by forgiving ourselves?

# VII

# *Noiseless Working*

The best way of working in all directions of life, at home or outside, is noiseless working—a thing of which so little is thought by many, and which is so very necessary in creating order, harmony, and peace in life. Very often a person does little and speaks much about it. In doing every little thing one makes noise, and thereby, very often, instead of finishing a thing successfully, one attracts difficulties.

The first thing that is to be remembered in character building is to understand the secret and character of human nature. We must know that every person in the world has his own object in life, his own interest, and his own point of view, and he is concerned with himself. His peace is disturbed when you wish to interest him in your object of interest, if you wish to force upon him your point of view. However near and dear he may be to you, he is not pleased with it. Very few consider this; they wish to pour out their own troubles and difficulties upon someone standing next to them, thinking that, "Everyone has the same interest in my subject as I myself," and that, "Everyone has the same point of view as I, myself," and that, "Everyone will be glad to hear me."

There is a story told that a person began to speak to his new acquaintance about his ancestors. He continued so long that the patience of the hearer was thoroughly exhausted. In the end the hearer finished the story by telling the person who spoke to him, "When I do not care to know about my own ancestors, what do I care to know about your ancestors?"

There are many who are very enthusiastic to let their neighbors know about every cold and cough they had; every little gain or loss, however small, they would be glad to announce with drums and bugles. This is a childlike quality. This tendency shows a child soul. Sometimes such a tendency frightens away friends and helps foes.

With noisy working people accomplish little. Being attracted by their noise, ten more people come and interfere and spoil the work which one person could have easily finished. Noisiness comes from restlessness. And restlessness is the sign of *tamas*, the destructive rhythm. Those who have made any success in life, in whatever direction, it is by their quiet working. In business, in industry, in art, in science, in education, in politics, in all directions of life, the wise worker is the quiet worker. He tells about things when the time comes, not before. The one who talks about things before he has accomplished them is like a cook who announces the dishes through the whole neighborhood before they are cooked.

There is a story told in the East of an enthusiastic servant. The master had a headache, and he told the servant to go and fetch a medicine from the chemist. The servant thought it would not be sufficient only to bring medicine from the chemist. So he also made an appointment with the doctor, and on his way home he visited the undertaker. The master asked, "Why are you so late?" The servant said, "Sir, I have arranged everything." Enthusiasm is a great thing in life. It is creative, and it is a key to success. But too much of it sometimes spoils things.

The more wise a person, the more gentle he is in everything he does. A gentleman in the English language is a quiet man. There is a fable that a donkey went to a camel and said, "Uncle, we shall be friends; we shall go grazing together." The camel said, "Child, I enjoy my walks alone." But the donkey said, "I am most eager to walk with you."

The good-natured camel consented and they both went together. Long before the camel finished grazing, the donkey had finished and was eager to express itself. He said, "Uncle, I would like to sing, if you do not mind." The camel said, "Do not do such a thing, it will be a terrible thing for you and me both. I have not yet finished my dinner." But the donkey had no patience. He could not control his joy and began to sing. The husbandman, attracted by the singing, came with a long bamboo. The donkey ran away and all the thrashing fell upon the camel. When the next morning the donkey went again to invite the camel, the camel said, "I am too ill. My way is too different from your way; from today we shall part."

There is such a great difference between the quiet person and a noisy person. One is like a restless child, the other like a grown-up person. One constructs, the other destroys. Quiet working must be practiced in every way, in everything. By making much ado about nothing, one creates commotion, disturbance in the atmosphere, and useless activity without any result. One also sees noise in the tendency of exaggeration, when one wants to make a mountain of a mole hill. Modesty, humility, gentleness, meekness—all such virtues manifest in the person who works through life quietly.

\* \* \*

*Question: Are* jelal, jemal, *and* kemal *the same as* rajas, sattva, *and* tamas?
Answer: Yes, *jelal* is *rajas, jemal* is *sattva,* and *kemal* is *tamas.*

*Question: Have they not the slightest difference?*
Answer: Yes, there is a difference, but that is only a very little difference.

*Question: If* kemal *is inertia, does everything have a moment*

*of rest constantly, and if so, how often?*
Answer: Rest between life and the hereafter is what is called purgatory. So there is always a gap between actions. For instance, when a person takes two steps, there is a gap between them. Also between exhaling and inhaling. Therefore, in every moment, in every breath, there is a moment of *kemal*.

In breathing, after every three quarters of an hour, there comes a short time when the breath changes, and then also there is *kemal*. So during a certain time of the day, a person feels lazy, depressed, or confused, for that is the outcome of *kemal*. *Kemal* has no tendency to action. Certain days come in the week when a person with all his enthusiasm does not wish to work; that is *kemal*.

In some people's lives, *kemal* obsesses them; they do not see the way, they feel the whole life as a stillness, everything seems so still and without movement. This is a deplorable state, and it results in a kind of insanity; a person wants to commit suicide. In other forms of insanity there is an inclination to fight another; there is hope because there is action. The cause of this insanity is disorder of breath; if that person would breathe rightly, he would be cured. He requires balance in breath.

There is a good type of *kemal* also, and that is in equilibrium, which is to be seen in the sage. When the switch is closed, the electric light goes out. So when the sage brings out the *kemal*, he closes the switch, that means closes the action of mind for that time. He does it by his will; he needs the time of quiet. When one feels this inertia, the ordinary person must not give way, for it is like the death of the mind.

*Question: Must one not go against this inertia?*
Answer: No, it is no use to fight it. But give them some interest. The world has so many beautiful things in poetry, music, nature.

# VIII

# *Inquisitiveness*

There is one thing which belongs to human nature, and its origin is in curiosity, the curiosity which gives a desire for knowledge. When this tendency is abused, it develops into inquisitiveness. It is wonderful to think that at the root of all defects is a right tendency. And it is the abuse of it which turns it into a wrong tendency.

When we consider how little time we have to live on this earth, we find that every moment of our life is precious, and that it should be given to something which is really worthwhile. When this time is given to inquisitiveness, wanting to know about the affairs of another, one has wasted that time which could have been used for a much better purpose.

Life has so many responsibilities and so many duties. There is so much that one has to correct in oneself; there is so much that one has to undo in what one has done. There is so much to attend to in one's affairs and to make one's life right that it seems as if a person were intoxicated who, leaving all his responsibilities and duties, occupies his mind and engages his ears in inquisitiveness. Free will is given to attend to one's own duties, to gain one's own objects, to attend to one's own affairs. And when that free will is used in trying to find out about others, the weakness of others, the lacks of others, the faults of others, then one certainly abuses that free will.

Sometimes a person is inquisitive because of his interest in the lives of others. But very often a person is inquisitive because it is his illness. He may have no interest in the matter at all, only that he wants to satisfy himself by hearing and knowing about others. Self-knowledge is the ideal of the philosophers, not the knowledge of the lives of others.

There are two phases in the development of man: one phase when he looks at others, another phase when he looks at himself. When the first phase has ceased, and the next phase begun, then one starts his journey to the desired goal. Rumi says, "Trouble not about others, for there is much for you to think about yourself."

Besides this, it is a sign of great respect to the aged, and to those one wishes to respect, to show no tendency of knowing more than one is allowed to know. Even in such close relationships as parents and children, when they respect the privacy of one another they certainly show a great virtue. To want to know about another is very often a lack of trust. The one who trusts does not need to unveil, does not need to uncover what is covered. He who wishes to unveil something wishes to discover it. If there is anything that should first be discovered, it is the self.

The time that one spends in discovering others, their lives, their faults, their weakness, one could have just as well spent in discovering one's soul. The desire to know is born in the soul. Only, man should discern what he must do and what is worth knowing. There are many things not worth troubling about. When one devotes one's time and thought to trying to know what one need not know, one loses that opportunity which life offers to discover the nature and secret of the soul, in which lies the fulfilment of the purpose of life.

\* \* \*

*Question: You told us the other day there is not such a thing as sadness. But why did Christ say "My soul is full of sadness,"*

41

*and also "My father, why hast thou abandoned me!" Is this not*
*a tragedy? And is there not a tragedy in life?*
Answer: We must know above and beyond all, the master's
human side of life, his divine side apart. If the human side
were not human, then why did God send a message to
human beings by a man? Why should he not send it by
angels? Because a human being knows human beings,
because he knows human limitation. That is the most
beautiful side of the master's life. If he did not feel sadness,
how could he sympathize with others? If all were perfect,
why be born on earth?

The purpose is that from limitation we grow toward
perfection. If from childhood all were wise, why did we
come? Beauty is in acquiring wisdom by failure, mistake.
All suffering in life, all is worth while and all will
accomplish the purpose of our coming on earth.

# IX

# *Gossip*

It must be remembered that one shows the lack of nobleness in the character by his love for gossip. It is so natural, and yet it is a great fault in the character to cherish the tendency of talking about others. In the first place, it is a great weakness one shows when one passes remarks about someone behind his back. In the second place it is against what may be called frankness, and, besides, it is judging another, which is wrong according to the teaching of Christ, who says "Judge ye not, lest ye be judged."

When one allows this tendency to remain in one, one develops a love of talking about others. It is a defect which commonly exists. And when two people meet who have the same tendency, together they complete gossip. One helps the other, one encourages the other. And when something is supported by two people, it of necessity becomes a virtue, even if it were only for the time being.

How often man forgets that, although he is talking about someone in his absence, it is spoken in the presence of God. God hears all things and knows all things. The creator knows about his creatures, about their virtues and faults. God is as displeased by hearing about the fault of his creature as an artist would be displeased on hearing bad remarks made by anyone on his art. Even though he acknowledged the defect of his art, still he would prefer finding it himself, not anyone else.

When a person speaks against someone, his words may not reach the person but his feelings reach him. If he is sensitive he knows of someone having talked against him. And when he sees the person who has been talking against him, he reads all he has said in his face, if he be sensitive and of keen sight. This world is a house of mirrors. The reflection of one is mirrored upon another. In this world where so many things seem hidden, in reality nothing remains hidden; some time or other it rises to the surface and manifests to view. How few in this world know what effect it makes on one's own personality, talking ill of another—what influence it has on one's soul.

Not only is man's self within like a dome where everything he says has an echo. Within man's self there is an echo of all he says, but that echo is creative and productive of what has been said. Every good and bad thing in life one develops in one's nature by taking interest in it. Every fault one has, as long as it is small one does not note it, and so one develops the fault till it results in a disappointment.

Life is so precious—and it becomes more and more valuable as one becomes more prudent—and every moment of life can be used for a much greater purpose. Life is an opportunity, and the more one realizes this the more one will make the best of this opportunity which life offers.

# X

# *Generosity*

The spirit of generosity in nature builds a path to God; for generosity is outgoing, is spontaneous. Its nature is to make its way toward a wide horizon. Generosity, therefore, may be called charity of heart. It is not necessary that the spirit of generosity must be always shown by the spending of money. In every little thing one can show it.

Generosity is an attitude which one shows in every little action that he does toward people with whom he comes in contact in his everyday life. One can show generosity by a smile, by a kind glance, by a warm handshake, by patting the younger soul with a pat of encouragement, with a pat showing appreciation, with that pat which expresses affection. One can show generosity in accommodating one's fellow man, in welcoming one's fellow man, in bidding farewell to one's friend; in thought, word, and deed, in every manner and form, one can show that generous spirit which is the sign of the *Wali*, the godly.

The Bible speaks of generosity by the word charity. But if I were to give an interpretation of the word generosity, I would call it nobility. No rank, position or power can prove one noble. Truly noble is he who is generous of heart. What is generosity? It is nobility, it is expansion of the heart. As the heart expands, so the horizon becomes wide, and one finds greater and greater scope in which to build the kingdom of God.

Depression, despair, and all manner of sorrow and sadness come from the lack of generosity. Where does jealousy come from? Where does aching of the heart come from? Where does envy come from? It all comes from the lack of generosity.

Man may not have one single coin to his name, and yet he can be generous, he can be noble, if only he has a large heart, a friendly feeling. The life in the world offers every opportunity to man, whatever be his position in life, to show if he has any spirit of generosity.

The changeableness and falsehood of human nature, besides the inconsideration and thoughtlessness that come out of those he meets through life, and furthermore the selfishness and grabbing and grafting spirit that disturbs and troubles his soul—this situation itself is a test and trial through which every soul has to pass in the midst of the worldly life.

If through this test and trial one holds fast to his principle of charity and treads along toward his destination, not allowing the influences that come from the four corners of the world to keep him back from his journey to the goal, he in the end becomes the king of life—even if at the end of his destination there is not one single earthly coin left to his name. It is not this earthly wealth that makes man rich. Riches come by discovering that gold-mine which is hidden in the human heart, out of which rises the spirit of generosity.

Someone asked the Prophet whose virtue was greater: the pious one who prays continually, the traveller who travels to make a holy pilgrimage, the one who fasts for nights and days, or the one who learns the scripture by heart. "None of them," said the Prophet, "is so great as the soul who shows through life charity of heart."

\* \* \*

*Question: Who is the greatest saint, the man who wills everything that God wills, or the one who has the greatest*

*sympathy with his fellow man?*
Answer: The latter.

*Question: Is there the same idea in the tale of the angel Iblis
and the angel Lucifer?*
Answer: Yes.

*Question: Is there any symbology veiled in the expression
"influences that come from the four corners of the world"?
What do you mean by this?*
Answer: From all sides.

*Question: If everything has its meaning, is there any reason
why the donkey's cry should be so terribly melancholy?*
Answer: It wants to show man that the sign of foolishness
is noise, and the sign of wisdom is quietude.

*Question: Is there any relation in the fact that the donkey has
a cross on its back?*
Answer: Yes, that is why the donkey has to take all the
burden on his back; it shows his resignation by submitting
his back to the will of his master.

*Question: And also with the fact that Christ rode on the back
of a donkey going to Jerusalem on Good Friday?*
Answer: That is the privilege of the server. The one who
serves, however humble, will have even the privilege of
serving God.

It is very difficult to know what makes one entitled
to privileges. Sometimes it seems that the most undeserving
become entitled to a privilege. There is a story of the
Prophet's passing to the other world. The day when
Muhammad was leaving this world he went to join the last
prayers at the mosque, and after the prayers were finished
he gave an address. In that address he mentioned that the
call had come from above, that he had fulfiled his mission,

and that he had to leave. And it produced a great panic among his devotees. There were many who were greatly devoted to him. And he said if he had ever spoken at any time in the slightest degree to the displeasure of a person, that person may return it a hundredfold. Or if he had borrowed from anyone anything, they must ask him to return it to them, as he was on the journey. And if he ever had insulted anyone, he asked them to please return it a hundredfold, and if he had in any way done any hurt or harm of any kind, that he would like it to be done to him before he left. The devotion and respect that the disciples had for the Prophet was so great that, his asking for anything like this apart, they were all choked up; they had no words to express to the Prophet their gratitude.

But there was one man, unrefined, and yet ambitious, who stood up and said, "Prophet, I remember that one day yourself touched me with a whip; and as it is your order, now I shall do it." The Prophet said, "I do not remember, but I am very glad, you may do it ten times more." And the panic was still greater in the mosque. And this man came with his whip near the Prophet, and said, "It was on my bare back." So the Prophet had to remove his shirt. Instead of whipping, he kissed the back of the Prophet, because he had believed that there was a seal of Prophetship on his back. It was his belief, and in order to have that privilege, he had to make up that story. It was arrogance outwardly, but devotion inwardly. There are many privileges that one attains by methods seemingly wrong, but the devotion proves true, expressed in every form.

*Question: What is the meaning of the belief that when a glass breaks without any visible cause, it is the announcement of the death of a dear one who is far away?*
Answer: Very often it is true. Sometimes it is a thought form, sometimes it is a spirit influence, sometimes it is the

influence of death itself which has its vibratory action through all things. And if the glass happens to become the subject of such vibration, if the current falls upon that glass with intensity, certainly it breaks. But that does not mean that a person must always take that warning, if a glass is broken. That would be terrible.

*Question: I thought it was good luck.*
Answer: I would at least suppose that when a glass was broken, if one thought it was very lucky, it would avoid much ill luck.

# XI

# *Gratefulness*

Gratefulness in the character is like a fragrance in a flower. A person, however learned and qualified in his life's work, in whom gratefulness is absent, is void of that beauty of character which makes a personality fragrant.

Gratefulness is being conscious of every little deed of kindness that anyone does to us. If we answer it with appreciation, in this way we develop that spirit in our nature. And by learning this we rise to that state when we begin to realize God's goodness toward us, his divine compassion, for which we can never be grateful enough.

A great poet among Sufis, Sa'adi, teaches gratefulness to be the means of attracting that favor of the forgiveness and mercy of God upon ourselves in which is the salvation of our soul. There is much in life that we can be grateful for, in spite of all the difficulties and troubles of life. Sa'adi says, "The sun and moon and the rain and clouds all are busy to prepare your food for you." And it is unfair indeed if you do not appreciate it in thanksgiving.

God's goodness is something that one cannot learn to know at once. It takes time to understand it. But little actions of kindness which we receive from those around us we can know, and we can be thankful, if we want to be. In this way man develops gratefulness in his nature, and expresses it in his thought, speech and action as an exquisite form of beauty. As long as one weighs and measures and says, "What I have done for you and what you have done for me," and "How kind I have been to you and how good you have been to me," he wastes his time over something which is inexpressible in words. Besides, by this he closes that fountain of beauty which rises from the stream of gratefulness.

The first lesson in the path of thankfulness that we can learn is to forget absolutely what we do for another; remember only what the other person has done for us. Throughout the whole journey on the spiritual path, the main thing that is to be accomplished is the forgetting of our false ego. In this way, we may arrive in some way at the realization of that being whom we call God.

There is a story of a slave called Ayaz, who was brought before the king with nine others, and the king had to select one to be his personal attendant. The wise king gave into the hands of each of the ten a wine glass and commanded them to throw it down. Each one obeyed the command. Then the king asked each one of them, "Why did you do such a thing?" Each of them answered, "Because your Majesty gave us the order," the plain truth, cut and dried. And then the tenth one, Ayaz, came near. He said, "Pardon me, king, I am sorry." He knew that the king already knew that it was his command. So by telling him, "Because you told me," there is nothing new said to the king.

This beauty of expression won the king so that he selected him to be his attendant. It was not long before he won the trust and confidence of the king, who gave him charge of his treasury in which precious jewels were kept. This made many jealous of the sudden rise of Ayaz from a slave to a treasurer of the king, a position which many envied.

No sooner did people know that Ayaz had become a favorite of the king than they began to tell numerous stories about Ayaz in order to bring him into the disfavour of the king. One of the stories was that every day Ayaz went in that room where the jewels were locked in the safe and that he was stealing them, every day, little by little. The king answered, "No, I cannot believe such a thing. You have to show me."

They brought the king as Ayaz entered this room, and made him stand in a place where there was a hole, to look into the room, and the king saw what was going on there. Ayaz entered this room and opened the door of the safe. And what did he take out from it? His old ragged clothes which he had worn as a slave. He kissed them and pressed them to his eyes and put them on the table. There incense was burning; this which he was doing was something sacred to him.

He then put his clothes on himself, looked at himself in the mirror and said to himself, as one might be saying a prayer, "Listen," he said, "O Ayaz, see what you were one day before. It is the king who has given you the charge of this treasury. So regard this duty as your most sacred trust and this honour as your privilege, and love the kindness of the king. Know that it is not your worthiness that has brought you to this position. Know that it is his greatness, his goodness, his generosity which has overlooked your faults, and which has bestowed that rank and position upon you by which you are now being honored. Never forget, therefore, your first day, the day when you came to this town. And it is the remembering of that day which will keep you in proper pitch."

He then took off the clothes and put them in the same place of safety, and came out. As he stepped out, what did he see? He saw that the king, before whom he bowed, was waiting eagerly to embrace him. The king told him, "What a lesson you have given me, Ayaz."

It is this lesson we all must learn, whatever be our position. Before that king in whose presence we all are slaves, let nothing make us forget that helplessness through which we were reared and we were raised, and that we were brought to life to do and to understand and to live a life of joy.

* * *

*Question: Will you please explain what you mean when you speak of listening to music spiritually? Can one listen to common music such as tunes played on a street organ?*
Answer: But we do not sit and meditate in the street. Besides, there is a technical stage; as a person develops in technique, in appreciating a better music, so he feels disturbed by a wrong, lower kind of music. But then there is a spiritual way which has nothing to do with technique. It is only to tune oneself with the music, and therefore the spiritual person is not concerned about its grade. No doubt, the better the music, the more helpful it is to a spiritual person; the higher the music, the better. But at the same time you must remember that there are Lamas of Tibet who make their concentration or meditation by moving a kind of rattle, the sound of which is not especially melodious. But at the same time they cultivate that sense of appreciation which raises a person by the help of vibrations on the higher planes. No doubt, there is nothing better than music for the upliftment of the soul.

*Question: What is the highest perception of freedom?*
Answer: The highest perception of freedom comes when a person has freed himself from the false ego, when he is no longer what he was. All manner of freedom, for the moment, gives a sensation of freedom. The true freedom is in oneself; when one's soul is free, then there is nothing in this world that binds us. Everywhere one will breathe freedom, in heaven and on earth.

*Question: Is it ungenerous to be critical in one's appreciation of things that do not agree with one's sense of beauty?*
Answer: When we are developing our sense of beauty, then

naturally we shall be critical of that which does not come up to our standard of beauty. But when we have passed that stage, then the next cycle of our evolution shows us a different experience; in that the divine compassion is developed. And therefore one becomes able, so to speak, to add to all that lacks beauty, and thus to turn all into perfection, which is the contemplation of the soul.

*Question: You said once that to repeat an expression of thanks did not make it stronger. But is it not a tendency of a grateful heart to repeat?*
Answer: Certainly it is. If I said that, it was said in a sense that one may make it a kind of mechanical thing. Very often people use "thank you" so bountifully that it almost loses its meaning. But the meaning of the word *namaz* in Sufism, which means prayer, is the repeating of thankfulness. What it does is bring to one's soul one's own voice, and the voice echoes once again before God, who is within ourselves. Therefore, the saying of the prayer is more powerful than only thinking on the subject. It is like thinking of a song and singing it—there is a vast difference between [the two]. By singing there is a satisfaction of the appetite. By thinking only, there is not.

*Question: What is the difference between thinking of a melody and singing it?*
Answer: Thinking the melody has half an effect upon the soul, and singing makes it complete, its full effect. But singing with thought makes it ten times more [effective], because a person may be there but his mind is somewhere else, not thinking of the song.

*Question: The difficulty is to always sing a melody and to keep the thought?*
Answer: By singing you can retain the thought more than by not singing and just wanting to keep the thought. It

helps the concentration a great deal.

*Question: Is it a distinct disadvantage for a human being to be born without a good ear?*
Answer: It is, because what is received through the ears goes deeper into the soul than by any other form. Neither by smelling or tasting or seeing does beauty enter so deeply into oneself as by hearing.

# XII

# *The Art of Personality*

It is one thing to be man and it is another thing to be a person. Man becomes a person by making a personality, by completing the individuality in which is hidden the purpose of man's coming on earth. Angels were made to sing the praise of the Lord; jinns to imagine, to dream, to meditate; but man is created to show humanity in his character. It is this which makes him a person.

There are many things difficult in life, but the most difficult of all things is to learn and to know and to practice the art of personality. Nature, people say, is created by God, and art by man. But really speaking, in the making of personality it is God who finishes his divine art. It is not what Christ taught which made his devotees love him. They dispute over those things in vain. It is what he himself was; it is that which is loved and admired by his devotees. When Jesus Christ said to the fishermen, "Come here, I will teach you to be fishers of men," what does it mean? It means: I will teach you the art of personality which will become as a net in this life's sea—for every heart, whatever be its grade of evolution, will be attracted by the beauty of the art of personality.

What is mankind seeking in another person? What does one expect in one's friend? He wants him rich, of a high position, of great power, of wonderful qualifications, or wide influence; but beyond and above all, he expects from his friend the human qualities—that is, the art of personality. If one's friend lacks the art of personality, all the above said things are of but little use and value to him.

There is a question: how are we to learn the art of personality? We learn it by our love of art, by our love of beauty in all its various aspects. The artist learns his art by his admiration of beauty. When a person gets an insight into beauty, then he learns the art of arts, which is the art of personality. Man may have a thousand qualifications or rank or position, man may possess all the goods of the earth, but if he lacks the art of personality he indeed is poor. It is by this art that man shows that nobleness which belongs to the kingdom of God.

The art of personality is not a qualification. It is the purpose for which man was created, and it leads man to that purpose in the fulfilment of which is his entire satisfaction. By this art, man not only satisfies himself, but he pleases God.

This phantom play on the earth is produced for the pleasure of that king of the universe whom the Hindus have called Indra, before whom Gandharvas sang and Upsaras danced. The interpretation of this story is that every soul's purpose is to dance at the court of Indra. It is to learn to dance at the court of Indra perfectly, which is, really speaking, the art of personality. The one who says, "But how can I dance, I do not know how to dance," defeats his purpose. For no soul is created to stand aside and look on. Every soul is created to dance at the court of Indra. The soul who refuses certainly shows its ignorance of the great purpose for which this whole play is produced on the earth.

\* \* \*

*Question: Will you please tell us if vaccination is desirable?*
Answer: Well, all things are desirable if they are properly used, and all are undesirable when they are abused. In point of fact, vaccination is the same spirit which is taught by Shiva, Mahadeva, as Hatha Yoga. It is said of Mahadeva

that he used to drink poison, and by drinking poison he got over the effect of poison. Mahadeva was the most venturous among the ascetics; that one can see by his wearing the serpent around his neck. Now, would you like to do it? If one can be so friendly with a serpent as to keep it around the neck, I think one can sit comfortably in the presence of someone one does not like. Hatred, prejudice, nervousness in the presence of someone we do not like will not come if one can take [on] a serpent; if one can take the bitter bowl of poison and drink it, which is against nature. When the soul has once fought its battle with all things that make it fear and tremble, shrink back and run away, that soul has conquered life, it has become the master of life, it has attained the kingdom.

Of course, the methods Mahadeva adopted are extreme methods; no one can recommend them to his pupil in this modern world, where there is fear, and vaccination comes from there: it is partaking of that poison which we fear, which might come someday in some form; one might breathe it in the breath or take it in the water or from the food, those same germs might come and enter one's body.

I have heard from a friend that a man in Switzerland has worked most of his life in getting the germs of consumption, tuberculosis, in order to inject them in cases where they can be cured; and he has had a great degree of success. Of course, such new methods may meet with a great deal of opposition, but at the same time the principle behind it has a very strong reason. This brings us to a much higher realization and a greater conception of life. It causes us to think that even what we call death, if that death were put into a cup and given to us to drink, that would bring us to life.

*Question: The Vedanta speaks of fourteen* lokas. *What is a* loka *and what is* pata loka *?*
Answer: These fourteen planes of existence are a

conception of metaphysics. The Sufi calls them *chauda tabq,* and they are the experience, fourteen different experiences, which consciousness has by the help of meditation. And *pata loka* is the lower plane, or the lowest plane.

*Question: Are these* lokas *divided over the seven planes?*
Answer: Not in the angelic or in the *jinn* [plane]. But in the experience of these fourteen planes the *jinn* and angelic *loka*s also are touched.

*Question: The Greeks say that sometimes a soul, fitted for a more perfect instrument, by a mistake connected itself with an animal body instead of with a human body. Is that so?*
Answer: The mistake follows the soul everywhere, wherever it goes; it never leaves it alone. It is there, whether on the earth or on the *jinn* plane.

*Question: Is it not strange that God should create this whole universe in order to hear his own praise? Is God not too great to want to hear his own praise?*
Answer: No, it is not the praise which God wishes to hear. The praise of God is the prescription for man, that by this pre-scription man comes to that sense which brings him nearer to God. In other words, by praising God man finishes that art in which is the fulfilment of the soul's coming on earth.

*Question: What is the best manner for an artist to receive inspiration: by waiting, by praying, or by continual working till inspiration comes back?*
Answer: By doing all three things together. One can wait while doing the work just the same. One need not put the brushes aside and wait, but do the work at the same time. One need not go into a corner and pray for inspiration, but do it while working, all at the same time.

*Question: Whom do you mean by Indra?*

Answer: In this respect it is God himself. It is a picture. For every *manvantara* there is a *Bodhisattva* and one *Manu. Bodhisattva* is *Nabi,* and *Manu* is the *Rassul.* These are names of man, although each of these words has a certain significance. *Manu* is the one who has touched the boundaries of human perfection. It is reaching the heights of man's perfection that is *Rassul* and *Maitreya;* these names are very significant: *Manu* has proved in his life to be a friend to every man he has met. The next is to prove to be a friend to God, that is *Rassul,* the fulfilment, where he has proved to be a friend to every soul. It is the perfection of friendliness in which is all spiritual perfection, when the spirit of friendliness is so developed that he is a friend to all. He cannot say, "There is one person in the world I cannot bear, whom I hate." When he has passed to that stage, his name is on the spiritual records.

*Bodhisattva,* the word, signifies the wise, wisdom, the boundary of wisdom, the perfection of wisdom where two opposite poles become one, where the serpent takes its tail in its mouth, which is the symbol of wisdom. It is therefore that the wise agree with all, with the wise and foolish both.

# XIII

## *Gentleness*

Every impulse has its influence upon the word and upon the action; and, therefore, naturally every impulse exerts its full power through words and deeds, unless it is checked. There are two types of persons: those who have acquired the power of checking their word and action when it would exert its full power and express itself with abruptness; the other kind of persons are those who mechanically allow this natural course of impulse to show itself in their word and deed, without giving any thought to it. The former, therefore, is gentle, and the latter is man.

Gentleness is the principal thing in the art of personality. One can see how gentleness works as the principal thing in every art: in painting, in drawing, in line and color; it is gentleness which appeals the most to the soul. The same we shall see in music. A musician may be qualified enough to play rapidly and may know all the technique, but what produces beauty is his gentle touch.

It is gentleness, mainly, which is all refinement. But where does it come from? It comes from consideration, and it is practiced by self-control. There is a saying in the East, "The weaker the person, the more ready to be angry." The reason is that this person has no control over his nerves. It is often lack of control over oneself which is the cause of a lack of gentleness. No doubt, one learns gentleness by consideration. One must learn to think before saying or doing. Besides, while saying or doing one must not forget the idea of beauty; one must know that it is not enough to say or do, but it is necessary to say or do everything beautifully.

It is the development of the nations and races which is expressed in gentleness; also it is the advancement of the soul's evolution which expresses itself in gentleness. Nations and races, as well as individuals, will show backwardness in their evolution if they show a lack of gentleness.

At this time of the world's condition it seems that the art of personality has been much neglected. Man is intoxicated with the life of avarice. And then the competitive spirit that exists, helped by the commercialism of the day, keeps man busy in acquiring the needs of his everyday life. The beauty which is the need of the soul is lost to view. Man's interest in all things of life—science, art, philosophy—remains unfinished in the absence of the art of personality. How rightly this distinction has been made in the English language: man and gentleman.

* * *

*Question: You spoke of Mahadeva as the chief of the ascetics; was he not a divine incarnation?*
Answer: Certainly he was.

*Question: Will you please tell us what we so admire in the beauty of the lion and tiger; they are not gentle.*
Answer: We admire them when they are in the cage. We would not admire them if they were at liberty. You must remember that very often very good reports come in the newspapers about beautiful looking Zeppelins; they looked so beautiful at night in the sky; also reports of how nicely the German army marched.[12] They admired it. Were they only admired? So we admire the tiger and lion. But we would have admired them still more if they had been gentle.

62

*Question: If the angelic world is the same as what is called* Buddhi *in terms of Vedanta, what is it that the Vedantist calls* Atma?

Answer: *Buddhi* is quite another word. *Buddhi* is not necessarily a plane. *Buddhi* is intelligence, reason, sense. *Atma* is the soul. The essential nature of the soul is *Buddhi,* the essence of reason, purest intelligence. Does the soul not pass the astral world coming from the jinn world? Just now I am not giving the terms of other expressions. I have only used these terms jinn and angel in order to simplify what I have to say about manifestation. Therefore, it would not be good to mix up these ideas which have been given to you with names of many different planes which can be afterwards explained to you.[13]

*Question: Is gentleness not the greatest power?*

Answer: Yes, gentleness is a power like the power of water. Water is powerful, and yet if there is a rock in the way the stream of water is going, it will surround the rock, it will not break it. It will make its way by the side, for the water is pliable, and so is gentleness.

*Question: But what if people will not listen to gentleness?*

Answer: Then we must talk to them in their own language. But only if it is necessary. If we can avoid it, it is still better. Gentleness, in the long run, will always prove the thing. But if we cannot manage, only in that case, we can learn that language. There is no objection in learning a language, is there?

*Question: Does Parvati stand for a quality, or was she a real woman?*

Answer: She was a real woman, Mahadeva's wife; she also stands for the property of *purusha.*[14]

*Question: Will you tell us something about the use of asceticism*

*in the spiritual life?*
Answer: I think that every person who is spiritually inclined, and in whom spirituality is innate, and who is to accomplish something worthwhile in the spiritual line, is born with more or less an ascetic inclination. There may be one person born with a greater inclination than another. But there is some inclination of asceticism in every soul born for spirituality. And now the question, what are the qualities of an ascetic? Independence, indifference, a love of solitude. He is self-sufficient, stern, egoistic, proud, celibate, contemplative, dreamy, visionary, retiring, thoughtful and wise. And here, I have said all his good and bad qualities.

*Question: Is egoistic among the bad qualities?*
Answer: In the end it comes right just the same.

*Question: How can one be egoistic and wise both?*
Answer: Well, there are many kinds of egoistic people. There are good points and bad points. Egoistic is selfish, and selfishness can produce cruelty, tyranny, injustice and dishonesty. Another side to the egoistic person is pride and independence and indifference, which gives him contentment. And besides this, the real egoistic person before whom there is his ego, when he watches that ego, which is first a statue of rock, after some time it becomes a living being. It comes to life. It becomes the very object after which one is seeking. And therefore the right egoistic person is right; it is the wrong egoistic person who is wrong.

*Question: Would you say that there is a time for everything in the spiritual life?*
Answer: Yes, a time for everything, that is so.

*Question: Someone who is egoistic is always hurting someone.*
Answer: That is the wrong side of the ego. There are

64

different stages of the ego. In different stages different things are right. The same thing which is wrong once, is right another time.

There are certain attributes which are spoken of by a great poet and a composer, Alias, and which show the qualities of a great soul: continual contemplation; the dignity of name, and respect of the position; taking the side of those who surrender; lifting up those who are standing at the bottom of the earth; giving merit to those who are talentless; giving knowledge to those who are without; providing for those who are without supply (such as medicine for the sick); whose presence clears away depression; who gives honor to those whom no one would honor; protecting those who are without protection; being constructive by influencing everything they touch. It is such souls in whom God may be found.

# XIV

# *The Persuasive Tendency*

There is a tendency hidden behind human impulse which may be called the persuasive tendency; it may manifest in a crude form and it may be expressed in a fine form. In the former aspect it is a fault, and in the latter aspect it is a mistake.

When crudely expressed, one urges another to agree with him, or to listen to him, or to do as he wishes be done by fighting, by quarrelling, by being disagreeable. Often such a person by the strength of his will power, or by virtue of his better position in life, gets his wishes done. This encourages him to continue further in the same method, until he finds a disappointing outcome of his method, if he ever finds it.

The other way of persuading is a gentler way: by putting pressure upon someone's kindness, goodness, and politeness, exhausting thereby his patience and testing his sympathy to the last. By this, people achieve for the moment what they wish to achieve, but in the end the effect is the annoyance of all those who are tried by this persuasive tendency.

Does it not show that to get something done is not so hard as to be considerate of the feelings of others? It is so rare that one finds a person in the world who is considerate of another person's feeling, even at the sacrifice of getting his own desires done. Everyone seeks freedom, but for himself. If he sought the same for another, he would be a much greater person.

The persuasive tendency no doubt shows a great will power, and it plays upon the weakness of others, who yield and give in to it owing to love, sympathy, goodness, kindness, politeness. But there is a limit to everything. There comes a time when the thread breaks. A thread is a thread, it is not a steel wire; even a wire breaks if it is pulled too hard. The delicacy of the human heart is not comprehended by everyone. Human feeling is too fine for common perception. A soul who develops his personality, what is he like? He is not like the root or the stem of the plant, nor like the branches or leaves; he is like the flower, the flower with its color, fragrance, and delicacy.

\* \* \*

*Question: You told us on Saturday of the great refreshment derived during sleep. Many distinguished men, as Napoleon for example, have performed a great amount of work on very little sleep. Is this because of their ability to contact the higher planes during the waking state?*
Answer: Yes, when a person is fast asleep, when his body is resting and mind still, his soul is able to freely breathe, and it absorbs in itself all the energy and vitality that is necessary for his whole being.

*Question: How is it that one recognizes, in a flash sometimes, a place or a scene that one has never visited before?*
Answer: The human body is a living wireless station. If only his senses and his mind were open to receive, he would not only receive all that comes from the world around him, but also from the world above him, in other words within him. And so every such experience as hearing something, or seeing something, or perceiving a fragrance, a depression without reason, or laughter without a cause—all these are the phenomena proving that man is the living wireless.

*Question: If the matter in bodies is always changing, would a person feel anything when an accident happens to the first person?*[15]

Answer: Not really, there is no connection in the matter. There would be only a kind of little attraction, such as there is in a blood relationship, a kind of attraction. But even that does not manifest to knowledge. It is a natural attraction, one does not know it. There is a very well-known story in *Shahnamah*[16] which explains this. There was a young man of whose ancestry a great ancient king of Persia knew. And he brought up this young man with great care and made him a most qualified wrestler, and his name was Rustam. This wrestler became the champion of the country and was trying to be a world champion, and he was very promising in his youth. He was kept by the king in reserve; he was not to see people, talk with people, mix with people. There came many wrestlers, and he won, this youth.

But the custom of that time was that, among two wrestlers, the one who is defeated, must acknowledge his defeat. And if he does not acknowledge, then he must be killed. And there came a world champion, and the king wanted this young man to fight with this world champion. And they fought. In the end the world champion brought this young man under him, and he was defeated. But the young man was very proud; he would not acknowledge his defeat. And therefore this world champion had to kill him. And when the knife had pierced through his throat, while bleeding he had a little sense and he said, "Remember, you have killed me, but some day you will meet my father and certainly he will win success over you."

This world champion asked his name. He said, "Rustam." The world champion went mad when he heard his name. This young man happened to be his son. All the time they fought there was an attraction; and yet the father did not know the son and the son did not know the father. To the mind there is a silent attraction, but it is not clear,

68

because it is matter.

*Question: What is it that accounts for the fact that when two people meet for the first time they feel they know each other? Is it the same thing?*
Answer: Yes. The only difference between the spirit and matter is, the divine intelligence pouring out directly is the spirit, and radiated through a dense medium is matter. Therefore, either in spirit or in matter there is divine intelligence just the same.

There has been a talk about the excavation in Egypt, that people should have felt agitated and angry against this. It is not so. The souls have much better occupation than to think about their body. Just as when one's nails are cut, one does not think of the nails any more. There is no link any more. If one keeps it all the time in his mind, there may be a little thought. It is the thought that keeps the connection. But the possibility of the same kings who are being excavated [knowing about it] is through the minds of those who do the work; that is the medium, because they are conscious of what they are doing. It is through that medium they can know that something is being done to their body.

There are strange stories told in India about snakes guarding the place where money was buried, because in the ancient times they used to dig under their house and put money there when going to travel. They did not want to tell anybody about it. Then they died and the thought was with the person who was dead. In order to protect that, when there was no other person there, the snakes were inspired to be there and guard it. Because that guarding tendency of the man who is gone is still in the serpent and the serpent is guarding it: one thing reflected upon another.

Then there are mothers very often having left their young children with the thought of protection. There has always been that reflection of the thought of protecting the children, that either among the relatives or friends, at once, as if an intuition or an innermost desire springs up in their heart to take charge of those children, and they have proved as kind as mothers. Because the mother's love was reflecting upon the heart of someone capable of protecting, it protects them.

*Question: Is the serpent chosen to guard?*
Answer: No, there is no choice, it just happens. But in the case of the mother, there sometimes is choice.

*Question: Where does the motive come from?*
Answer: The prophetic idea rises above philosophical analysis. Because the Prophet says it is God who is merciful and compassionate; and all children are his children, whether to their mother or to someone else they give their heart. Therefore, there is no need to distinguish the motive, because in reality all motives belong to One, and that is God. But of course that is the ideal side. On the philosophical side there is a distinction. But I should think that either guided by anybody or obsessed, an act of kindness and a service of love is always a virtue. Because after a study of metaphysics or philosophy, after reading or meditating, or after living like a saint, or after accomplishing all that a master may accomplish, in the end one thing a person learns out of all that he has studied—and that is to serve another. There is all religion, philosophy, and mysticism in that, and if one has not learned that, he has not learned anything.

There are wealthy people with millions, and there are people of rank who are in high positions, and there are mighty magicians with great power, and yet they all will prove to be poor and useless in the end compared with the one who is always ready to do what he can for his fellow man. In this is the essence of the whole learning, the whole spirituality and mysticism: how can we be useful, how can we be serviceable to the person next to us?

# XV

# *Vanity*

The whole manifestation is the expression of that spirit of the *logos*, which is called, in Sufi terms, *kibria*. Through every being, this spirit manifests in the form of vanity, pride, or conceit. Had it not been for this spirit working in every being as the central theme of life, no good or bad would have existed in the world, nor would there have been great or small; all virtues and every evil is the offspring of this spirit. The art of personality is to cut the rough edges of this spirit of vanity which hurt and disturb those one meets in life. The person who talks of "I," as many times as he talks about it, so much more he disturbs the mind of his listeners.

Vanity expressed in rigidity is called pride; when it is expressed nicely it is termed vanity. Often people are trained in politeness, and they are taught a polished language and manner. Yet, if there be this spirit of vanity pronounced, in spite of all good manners and beautiful language it creeps up and sounds itself in a person's thought, speech, or action, calling aloud, "I am, I am." If a person be speechless, his vanity will leap out from his expression, from his glance. It is something which is the hardest thing to suppress and to control.

The struggle in the life of adepts is not so great with passions or emotions, which sooner or later by more or less effort can be controlled, but with vanity; it is always growing. If one cuts down its stem, then he lives no more, for it is the very self, it is the "I," the ego, the soul or God

71

within. It cannot be denied its existence, but only struggling with it beautifies it more and more and makes more tolerable that which in its crude form is intolerable.

Vanity may be likened to a magic plant. If one saw it in the garden growing as a thorny plant, and if one cut it off, it would grow in another place in the same garden as a tree of fruits. And when one cuts it away, in another place in the same garden it will spring up as a plant of fragrant roses. It exists just the same, but in a more beautiful form, and would give happiness to those who touch it. The art of personality, therefore, does not teach us to root out the seed of vanity, which cannot be rooted out as long as man lives. But its crude outer garb may be destroyed, that after dying several deaths it might manifest as the plant of desire.

*  *  *

*Question: Is there any other way of changing the object of desire than that of satiety? I mean for the man in the world?*
Answer: Yes, which is by rising above it. For instance, that person has no virtue of fasting who is not hungry. Fasting is a virtue for that person who feels inclined to eat, and who renounces food.

*Question: Might not vanity be called self-admiration?*
Answer: Certainly.

*Question: Can vanity be rooted out?*
Answer: Vanity is life itself, and so its existence cannot be denied.

*Question: What is the Vedantic equivalent of* Kibria?
Answer: It is "Om."

*Question: In* Mysticism of Sound[17] *it is said: "It is the reflection of the sun in the moon which makes the moon appear*

*round like the sun." Do you mean by this that the moon is round because the sun is round?*
Answer: All celestial bodies are round, because they are the reflections of the sun. If the sun were square all would have been square.

*Question: Will you please tell us more about the relationship between the sun and the moon, and how they work together?*
Answer: The moon is the complement to the sun, and the contrary. One positive, one negative. One *jelal*, one *jemal*. The moon responds, the sun expresses. And so it is the power of affinity between the sun and the moon, which is a power that holds the cosmos. But the sun is again the reflection of the divine sun, a physical reflection; as the moon and planets are a reflection of the sun, so the sun is a reflection of the divine sun, which is obscure to the physical eyes.

*Question: What do you mean by reflection in that sense? Do you mean it in the same sense that they reflect the light of the sun?*
Answer: Yes, they are respondent bodies. For instance, the crystal is a body which is respondent to the light; so are the planets to the sun, and the sun to the divine manifestation. Therefore, the sun in all ages has been taken as a sign for the worship of God.

*Question: Will you tell us please the difference between the master and the murshid?*
Answer: The master or the saint are the paths of those who tread the spiritual path, the high initiates. The *murshid* is what the Hindus call a *guru*, a teacher, whom the pupils accept as their guide on the spiritual path, and from whose hands they take their initiation.

*Question: One being can also be all these beings?*

Answer: Yes.

*[Question missing]*
Answer: What is the path? The path is the vacuum. When a person has removed himself then there is a vacuum. As long as a person is stating "I am," so long he is a stone in his own path. When he has removed himself, then he is the path, then he is the vacuum. What everyone is seeking is the true ego, which is God. When the false ego is removed then there is no end to what he becomes.

*Question: Is the moon the eye of God?*
Answer: Yes, it is the left eye of God; the right eye is the sun.

*Question: Has the arrangement of the stars in the constellations any definite purpose, any spiritual purpose?*
Answer: Yes, they all have their part to perform in the cosmos. And the influence that each planet has upon different souls, that makes a great link between the condition of that star and the soul; and every move that that particular star makes has its influence on those connected with that star. This is the key to the secret of the spiritual hierarchy, that influence of *Wali, Ghous, Qutub, Nabi, Rassul* is considered as the influence of the sun, the moon, the planets and stars. And that every change that takes place in all the planetary system, that change has much to do with those who represent here on the earth that particular planet. That is what makes the spiritual hierarchy on the earth. And besides, as the stars and planets have their influence on the living beings, so the living beings who represent the planets, their influence is working upon the human beings just the same.

*Question: Is it wise to study astrology?*
Answer:  Study is always good, but it must not be so

harmful as putting one's faith in a limited condition. It is better for a sensitive person never to have his horoscope taken, either for himself or for his children, for the warnings are so retained in mind that they become true. It is wise for astrologers never to say bad things and always good things. Psychologically, it is always wrong to prognosticate bad things.

The seer sees much more than the astrologer can. For the seer the present and past and future is written just like a letter. Every person, every person's soul, is just like an open letter, written. But if he would begin to say it, then the sight would become dim, more and more every day, because it is a trust from God. If he would disclose it, this divine power would diminish little by little. With spiritual things, they are trusted to those who can keep them secret.

*Question: Would it ever be possible for a person for the love of power to betray it?*
Answer: Yes, it is possible. But that brings about terrible disasters. There is a story that there was a king, and he was travelling through different places, and it happened that he came into troubles, and he had to take the profession of a baker in order to get along for some time until he again could go to his place. When serving in the house of the baker, he made a little money so that he could go back to his kingdom. He was hiding from some difficulty. He told the baker one day, "You have been so very kind, now I will tell you that I am the king. But you must keep this as a secret." But the moment the baker heard, he said, "Ha!" And when he said "Ha", he got a kind of upset in his system; he was almost ill. He said, "Take me to the doctors, there is something wrong."

It was because he had no power to keep the secret. His wife came, his children. He said, "I am dying." He would not eat, he would not drink, not sleep, because there was no accommodation here to keep the secret. The secret was too great a secret for him to keep. The doctors could not do anything. He said, "Well, take me somewhere in the woods." They took him, and he said, "Now go away." Then he came to a tree, and he said to the tree, "I want to tell you something, listen: the person who came to my house to wash my dishes was a king." And as he said so he became better.

Then the story goes on that in that tree there was a ghost who listened to it, who could not keep the secret in his heart. He had to tell it to somebody. The ghost went to the same kingdom and obsessed someone, and the secret came out. And the king knew that nobody knew except the baker. He sent for the baker, and he came before the king. And the baker said, "I have never told any living being; I have only said it in the forest, because I was ill." But the king said, "But how did the secret come out?" Then they found that it was the ghost who told the secret.

This story tells that it is not everyone who can assimilate the drinking of the liquor of any intoxicating drink. Someone, to whom you just gave a little sip, becomes drunken; another, you can give one good glass. The one who becomes a seer, him God trusts. The prophets and messengers have first proved themselves in their lives by keeping the secret of their friends. They have kept the trust of all those, just like a safe. People came with their mistakes and difficulties; errors, sorrows they have poured out. It all went into their heart; it was safe, no one could look at it—more safe with the spiritual beings than with themselves.

The spiritual beings told them, "Do not tell another, as you have told me." They did not trust the people with their own secrets. When that is the capacity of the heart, then in the end God begins to trust: "You have become the trust of my creatures, now I give you my trust." It is the reward of that virtue. It shows the best quality in man when he can keep the secret.

# XVI

# *Self-Respect*

The consideration of dignity, which in other words may be called self-respect, is not something which can be left out when considering the art of personality. But the question, what is it and how may this principle be practiced?, may be answered that all manner of light-heartedness and tendency to frivolity must be rooted out from one's nature in order to hold that dignity which is precious to one. The one who does not care for it, he does not need to take trouble about it; it is only for the one who sees something valuable in self-respect. A person with self-respect will be respected by others, even regardless of his power, position, possessions, or rank. In every position or situation in life, that person will command respect.

There arises a question: has light-heartedness then any place in life, or is it not necessary in life at all? All is necessary, but everything has its time. Dignity is not in making a long face; respect is not in making cross brows. By frowning or stiffening of the body one does not get honor.

Dignity is not in being sad or depressed. It is only dividing one's activities according to their proper times. There are times for the laughter, there are times for seriousness. For the person who is laughing all the time, his laughter loses its power. The person who is always light-hearted does not command that weight in society which is necessary. Besides, light-heartedness often makes man offend others, without meaning to do so. The one who has no respect for himself has no respect for others. He may think for the moment that he is without regard for conventionalities and free in his expression and feeling, but he does not know that it makes him as light as a scrap of paper, moving hither and thither in space, taken by the wind.

Life is as a sea, and the further on the sea one travels, the heavier the ship one needs. So in this sea of life, for a wise man to make a life, there is a certain amount of weight required which gives balance to the personality. Wisdom gives that weight; its absence is the mark of foolishness. The pitcher full of water is heavy. It is the absence of water in the pitcher which makes it light, as one without wisdom is light-hearted. The more one studies and understands the art of personality, the more one finds that it is the ennobling of the character which is going forward toward the purpose of creation. All the different virtues, beautiful manners and beautiful qualities—they are all the outcome of the nobleness of the character. But what is nobleness of the character? It is a wide outlook.

* * *

*Question: Is dignity of position sometimes in opposition with kind impulses?*
Answer: When a person is on duty, it is better to follow the duty. For instance, when the judge is sitting upon the chair of the judge, and there is another person who is too weak to stand, the judge may be just as kind to say that a chair may be brought, not give his own chair; by that he would not be fulfilling his duty properly. When he is out of the court, then he can show his kindness.

*Question: Will you please tell us how it is that sometimes when people meet for the first time there is instinctive repulsion in them and yet afterwards they may become friends?*

Answer: It is not often so, perhaps sometimes. Because really those who are to be friends, they become friends at first sight. The first impression is, really speaking, a continual impression and that becomes more and more. But it is quite possible that sometimes something that had a repellent influence, if one can overcome it, one can bear it more easily; then one finds something more interesting in that person, then one becomes friends. It is only a matter of getting accustomed. A person who does not withstand because he is not accustomed to those vibrations, may by tolerance and endurance become accustomed; then he has conquered that weakness. It is the same as becoming accustomed to poison.

*Question: "Unto the woman he said, 'I will greatly multiply thy sorrow and thy conception; in sorrow thou shalt bring forth children.'" "And unto Adam he said, 'In the sweat of thy face shalt thou eat bread'".[18] But through all the ages women, except a few of the privileged ones, have had to work also in the sweat to gain their bread; so they have to bear a double burden. Is it not an injustice?*
Answer: There is not one injustice, there are numberless injustices. Only this was said long ago; now it would have been said differently. It only shows the duties of womanhood as existed before, that pertained to that idea. And the duties of man as existed before, that pertained to that. This does not belong to the present time.

*Question: Which is the quickest way to attain dignity? Dignity, by seeking to be dignified, by seeking truth which will give dignity, or is seeking dignity and truth the same thing?*
Answer: By learning to think one develops dignity in one's nature. The more thoughtful one becomes, naturally the more dignified one becomes, because dignity springs from thoughtfulness. A person who offends is light-hearted; and the one who is light-hearted is foolish. One may seem

clever and yet be light-hearted; but he goes no further than the worldly cleverness, and very often that cleverness falls at his feet as an iron chain. As Sa'adi says, "My cleverness, thou actest so often against me."

*Question: Sometimes an egoistic person is very dignified.*
Answer: The true dignity is always unconscious. It is a natural outcome of thoughtfulness. It may be that a person has dignity and at the same time he is egoistic. He has not yet risen above the ego, because it is the greatest difficulty to conquer the ego. Egoism causes lack of love; love is the first and the last, both, and all through.

*Question: What is love and how should one be loving?*
Answer: It is very difficult to say what is love and how one can be loving. Is it that one should be embracing or running after people or talking sweetly? What is it that one could show to be loving, because every person has a different way of expressing his love. Perhaps there is someone who has a love hidden in his heart; it does not manifest. With another it comes out in his words, actions. For another, perhaps, it rises just like the vapors and charges the whole atmosphere. For another, it is like a spark in the stone: outside the stone is cold, inside there is a spark. Therefore, to judge who has love and who has not is not the power of every person. It is very difficult.

For instance, love as a fire rising from a cracker, calls out "I am love!" and burns up and then is finished. There is also a fire in the pebble which never manifests. If one holds the pebble, it is so cold; at the same time it is there, some day you can strike it, and it is there. And as many people as there are, so [love has] as many different qualities. One cannot judge the love of one person, or the other, because the manner of expressing love for every person is different.

When we ask the followers of other religions, for

instance, they have a thousand things to say against the religion of their adversaries. Not only about the religion, but also about the prophet. It is not only because they are of another religion that they will find fault with the very prophet, who is perhaps the prophet of millions of people; a person can easily find fault with him, and may have quite a reason to find fault. Therefore, no man has ever been born on earth who may be called perfect in every way. Except you can say it with regard to someone who has gone already from this plane of the earth, because he is not before you to be examined and tested again. And if man were perfect, then what would be the difference between man and God? Man is limited, God is perfect.

# XVII

# *Word of Honor*

A noble-minded person shows as something natural in his character an esteem for his word, which is called the word of honor. For that person, his word is himself. And it could increase to such an extent that even his life could be sacrificed for his word. A person who has reached this stage is not very far from God, for it is often mentioned in the scriptures, "If you wish to see us, see us in our words." If God can be seen in his words, the true soul can be seen in his words. Pleasure, displeasure, sweetness, bitterness, honesty, dishonesty, all these are to be discerned in the words man speaks. For the word is the expression of thought, and thought is the expression of feeling. And what is man? Man is his thought and feeling. So what is the word? The word is man's expression, the expression of his soul.

The man upon whose words you can rely, that man is dependable. No wealth of this world can be compared with one word of honor. The man who says what he means proves in this virtue spirituality. To a real person, to go back on his word is worse than death, for it is going backward instead of going forward. Every soul is going onward toward his goal, and the person who is really going onward shows it in his word.

At the present time, when it has been necessary to have so many courts and so many lawyers, which has in turn necessitated the keeping of so many prisons, which are flourishing [more] every day, this all shows the lack of that virtue which has been valued by the noble-minded ever since the beginning of civilization. For in this quality man shows his human virtue, a quality which neither belongs to the animals, nor is attributed to the angels.

What is religion? Religion, in the true sense of the word, is beyond explanation. It is a delicate thread too delicate to be touched, for it is too sacred to be touched. It is the ideal which could be polluted if it were touched, and this can be found in that sensitiveness which in other words may be called spirituality.

Out of regard for the word, many in this world have gone through sacrifices; sufferings and pains have been inflicted on them, but it was only to put their virtue to the test. For every virtue has to prove itself by going through a test of fire. When it has passed its trial it becomes a solid virtue. This can be practiced in every little thing one does in one's daily life. A person who one moment says one thing, and another moment another thing, even his own heart begins to disbelieve him.

The great ones who have come on the earth from time to time and who have shown many virtues, among them this virtue has been the most pronounced. Muhammad, before having come before the world as a prophet, was called "Amin" by his comrades, which means "trustworthy." The story of Harish Chandra is known to the Hindus down through the ages; the example that he has set is engraved upon the mind of the whole race. The story of Hatim, a Sufi among Zoroastrians, has been a great inspiration to the people of Persia. In whatever part of the world, and in whatever period, by the thoughtful and those with an ideal, the word of honor will be valued the most.

There is a man of history; it may be his name was Chava, I have forgotten. He was a Rajput, a Maharaja. There was a battle between that Maharaja and the Mogul emperor of Delhi, and this battle continued for a very long time. And while the emperor of Delhi made many other

Maharajas come to his court and bow, it was only this one Maharaja who said that as long as he lived he would never bow, and therefore he had to go through a great many sacrifices. His power was decreasing, but his mind power was increasing. But he was of a very fine nature, and a very high ideal, and he was very fond of poetry.

When this emperor became very disheartened after a long battle, he then told the brave men of his court in confidence that there would be a very big prize given to the one who would bring the head of this Maharaja, for this Maharaja had caused very great trouble and great expense. No one in the court seemed to take a vow readily that "I will do it," except a poet. He was a great poet of the court of the emperor. Everybody laughed at him, all the big warriors; they said they could not do it with their armies. This poet said he would do it.

This poet went to the court of the Rajput and his great talent made an impression upon the Rajput; and perhaps this was a moment of some planetary influence working, that he happened to say, "Ask, o poet, I really do not know what to give you. There seems to be nothing in my treasury that is equal to your knowledge. Ask, what do you want me to give you? What can please you?" "No, king," he said, "do not promise that." "No, once promised it is promised," said the king. The poet asked, "Will you keep it?" He said, "You do not need to ask, a promise is a promise." The poet said, "I feel very embarrassed to ask you, but it is your head that I want." He at once unsheathed his sword, put it in the hand of the poet and said, "Here it is, a very small thing you have asked; it is not greater than the word I have given."

His people, his children, his family, they were all upset. His ministers became very upset. He was not upset at all. He was in good spirits. He said, "I have promised, it must be given; here it is." The poet said, "Now as you have promised me your head, what are you to do with your body? Why not the body also? Come along with me." He said, "Yes." He walked behind the poet, the poet first, he after.

The poet brought him alive to the court of the emperor, and there was a great excitement in the whole court, thinking that for years and years they have battled. No one could bring him; yet here the poet brought him. In order to satisfy his vanity, the emperor asked the poet to bring him into the court. He should be brought as a prisoner. He was no prisoner, still he went where the poet took him. And the emperor looked at him, at that enemy with whom there was war for so many, many years, and he said, "You have come after all. But still it does not seem that your pride has gone, for you do not even think of bowing now that you have come to the court." He said, "Who must bow, a dead person? A dead person never bows. As long as he was living he never bowed. Now this is the dead body. Let anything be done with it. It is nothing."

No doubt the iron-hearted emperor overlooked that beauty which was shown by this Maharaja and said that he was to be beheaded. But the poet said, "No, emperor, if he is to be beheaded, I am the first to be killed." The emperor said, "No, this one!" "No," the poet said, "Me also, for I will never find another soul who will appreciate my merit as he has done. He has given his life." So the poet died with this Rajput. And the son of this poet, the whole family came; they were all so gifted and inspired, they were just like the salt of the soil. Everyone of them said one poem and died. The whole family of the poet was sacrificed for the sake of this Maharaja, in his appreciation of that merit and that great virtue that he had shown.

And though he passed through that suffering, yet there was no suffering. His ideal had gone through the test; he died that death of honor which has made the record of his merit. It is not only one case. In many cases you will find the noble souls who have proven themselves to be on the path of God and spirituality; they have shown it in their esteem of the word. Once their word was given, if the whole earth were upset, they would keep to it just the same.

* * *

*Question: Will you please tell us why in the Islamic religion, which teaches the divine unity, God speaks of himself as "us"?*
Answer: In the English language it can only be translated as "we" and "us," but it is the manner in which, in ancient times, the king spoke. And why? The king did not speak as a person, but as the nation; therefore, God speaks as the whole being, the whole creation. "Us" means all the souls that exist; all are included.

*Question: Is it better then to keep to one's word, even if one finds later that one was mistaken in giving it?*
Answer: It depends upon what it concerns. A mistake is a mistake. This question has nothing to do with the keeping of one's word. Keeping one's word is more like a promise. Besides this, a person speaks without thought when he has to change. But when a person makes the habit [of saying], "Yes, I spoke by mistake," then next time he will make another mistake. But if he will always try to speak, whatever he speaks, without [making a] mistake, then in time he will be able to do so without a mistake.

I mean, it is not easy always for everybody to become so thoughtful and wise that everything they say is without mistakes. Mistake is in the nature of man. But try to make it less and less; there must be the tendency of making fewer mistakes. But it all depends upon a person's evolution. There is a certain state of evolution when a person can maintain his word; another, where he cannot maintain his word, he is too weak to keep it. But by having the tendency, he will get that strength as he goes on, that desire and the esteem of the word. The more one alters, the more there is a tendency to alter, and the more one keeps, the more there is a tendency to keep it.

There was a very wonderful story of a girl, a Rajput girl born in Kashmir. She was playing with the little girls, somewhere around her house. And the Maharaja, the king of that place, happened to be walking about in her street disguised as an ordinary man to see the condition of his subjects. He happened to come near these girls talking to one another. They were very young. This girl was about eight or nine years old. And they were all talking about the doll's marriage. Then that conversation came to the Maharaja.

One of the girls happened to say, just unconsciously, when asked, "Who are you going to marry?" She said, "Maharaja," who was standing there. He was very amused. He was like her grandfather. Only he said to the parents of the child in a joke, "Now note it down, that when the marriage of this child will take place, the dowry must be given by the State as a gift of the Maharaja."

Soon after that the Maharaja died. And the girl grew up, and the time came for her marriage. But whenever there came a question of marriage, her words were, "I gave my word." People said, "The Maharaja has died, what do you say?" She said only, "I have given my word." That was all people heard from her, never another word. It seemed as if it was born with her, that honour of the word. The word that was given was given.

No doubt, an ideal is such a thing that one could go to an extremity; as it is said in the Sanskrit language, "The extremity of all things must always be avoided as undesirable." One might go too far in any kind of virtue. But at the same time ordinarily, it is not so. Ordinarily, one does not consider enough. For instance, one cannot be too good, one cannot; or in being true, one cannot be too true. The way that one can practice this is in one's everyday life, in every little thing one does, if one only thought, "What I have said, I must do, even if it be a very small thing."

"First was the word, and the word was God." So really, when breaking the word, one breaks God. For the one who realizes that, then in every word one speaks one can see God. When one sees God in it, then God begins to speak, because then God comes through the word of man. When man begins to realize this, then what he says becomes his religion. It too is sacred for him.

# XVIII

# *Graciousness*

No sooner has the soul touched the inner kingdom, which is the divine kingdom, than the true nobility of the soul becomes manifest from that soul in the form of graciousness. The kings and those belonging to the aristocratic families were trained in the manner of graciousness. But it is born in the heart of man. This means every soul shows the aristocratic manner from the moment it touches the inner kingdom. This shows that the true aristocracy is the nobility of the soul, when the soul begins to express in every feeling, thought, word, and action that graciousness which belongs to God himself.

Graciousness is quite different from that wrong manner which is termed in English patronizing. The gracious one, before expressing that noble attribute, tries to hide himself even from his own eyes. The reason why the great ones are gracious, the truly noble people, is because they are more sensitive to all the hurt or harm that comes to them from the unripe. And therefore, out of their kindness, they try to keep themselves back from doing it to another, however small in position.

There is a story of a dervish who was standing in the royal road at the moment when the procession of the king was passing. Happy in his rags as he was, he did not at all mind who was coming. He did not move an inch on the warnings of the people who were running before the procession, till they pushed him away. Yet he did not move very far; he only said, "That is why."

There came the bodyguards on horseback; they did not push him but said, "Away, away dervish, do you not see the procession coming?" The dervish did not move an inch but only answered, "That is why." Then followed the noblemen. They saw the dervish standing. They did not like to tell him to move; they moved their own horses instead. The dervish, seeing that, said, "That is why." Then arrived the chariot of the king. His eyes fell on the dervish standing in rags boldly in the middle of the road. Instead of waiting for his bow, the king bowed himself, and the dervish answered, "That is why."

There was a young man standing by his side. He could not understand the meaning of those words, "That is why," for every treatment. And when he asked the dervish to kindly explain what he meant by those words, "That is why," he said, "It explains all I mean."

There is a great truth in what Christ has said in the sermon on the mount, that "Blessed are the humble, for they will inherit the kingdom of the earth." This will always prove true, whatever be the time and evolution of the world. Be it the time of aristocracy, be it the period of democracy, the value of that nobility of nature which is expressed in graciousness will always command its price.

It is easy to know this word, but most difficult to practice it through life, for there is no end to the thought that needs to be given to every action in life. It wants judgement and the fair sense of weighing and measuring all one does. Besides that, it needs the fine sense of art and beauty, for in making the personality finished, one attains to the highest degree of art. Verily, the making of the personality is the highest art there is. The Sufi, whose life's object is to cultivate humane attributes, in which lies the fulfilment of the purpose of his life, considers this as his religion.

A young man one day showed a little impatience to his aged father, who at his age could not hear very clearly and had asked him two or three times to tell him again. Seeing the disturbed expression on his face, the father said, "My son, do you remember that there was a day when you were a little child and asked me what the bird was? And I said to you, 'the sparrow'. You perhaps asked me fifty times, and I had the patience to repeat it to you again and again, without being hurt or troubled about it. I was only pleased to tell you all I knew. Now, when I cannot hear you clearly, you can at least have patience with me if I did not hear you once, to explain it to me twice."

It seems that in order to learn that noble manner of life, what mostly is needed is patience, sometimes in the form of endurance, sometimes in the form of consideration, and sometimes in the form of forgiveness.

# XIX

# *Economy*

There is a sense and a tendency of economizing, more or less, to be found in every soul. And when this tendency works with those around one, and with those with whom one comes in contact, one develops one's personality. The desire to spare another, if one could, of exercising patience, instead of trying to test his patience to its utmost, is the tendency of economy, a higher understanding of economy—to try and save another, spare another, from using his energy in the way of thought, speech, and action; it all saves another his energy, and for oneself it is adding beauty to one's personality. A person ignorant of this in time becomes a drag upon others; he may be innocent, but he can be a nuisance, for he has neither consideration for his own energy, nor thought for the other's.

This consideration comes to one from the moment he begins to realize the value of life. As man begins to consider this subject, he spares himself from unnecessary thought, speech, or action, and economically he uses his own thought, speech, and action. And by valuing one's own life and action, one learns to value the same for others.

The time of human life on earth is most precious, and the more one practices economical use of that time and energy which is most precious, the more one knows how to make the best of life. Speaking apart, even hearing another speak is a continual tension. It robs one of his time and energy. When one cannot understand, or at least does not try to understand, something that can be said in one word, and wants it to be put in a sentence, he certainly has no sense of economy.

Economizing with one's money is of much less importance compared to economizing with one's life and energy, and that of others. For the sake of beauty, grace, dignity, and respect, when dealing with others one must go so far and no further. One cannot drive with the same whip a friend, an acquaintance, and a stranger. There again the question of economy must be considered. The person who is sensible enough to guard his own interest in life may be called clever. But the one who guards the interests of others even more than his own is wise, for in doing so he, without knowing, does things to his own advantage also. It is the same sense of economy which one uses with little things in one's everyday life at home and in business. That same sense used in a higher form of thoughtfulness and consideration makes one more capable of serving others, which is the religion of all religions.

* * *

*Question: Will you please explain where the balance is to be found in keeping your word or not? To say a promise is a promise seems to me a little rigid.*

Answer: It does not seem rigid to me; on the other hand, it seems most fine. When a person gives his word, it is his soul, it is his own being. And the greater importance he attaches to his word, the greater the person he becomes. What is the person? The person is his ideal. As high as his ideal is, so high is the person. If a person['s ideal] is something which he can move away with his shoes, it is nothing; it is like a football. A word is something like a jewel which is mounted on the crown of the king. The word is man's beauty, the radiance of his face. When it is lost, the radiance is gone. There are men who, when their word is lost, would not want to live any longer; life has become distasteful. There is something godly in it, something divine, because it is the divine spark which gives that sense. There is something living in it. Therefore, what we call promise in a word is not the word, it is the sense of honor. And I think that if there is anything by which you can test how high a person is, how fine his greatness, his goodness, that is the best way of testing him, by his word.

*Question: And circumstances may change?*
Answer: The circumstances always change, but God never changes. Why are we, with all the beauty that is in this world, the gems, jewels, and beautiful things, why are we seeking for something constant, reliable? We are looking for something that does not change.

*Question: Speaking of the playing of a part . . . capacity for concentration . . . .*
Answer: No, playing a part is the outer thing. If his inner being is unmoved, if he single-mindedly concentrates on a certain spot, then the outer part does not matter. But really speaking, what is the life of a mystic, of a God-realized man, if it is not playing a part? His life is nothing but playing the part; not one part, but a thousand parts. A part he has to play as a servant, as a master, as a friend, as a son of his parents, as a father of his children, as a neighbor of his neighbors—and yet in his mind he realizes that oneness of all, that love of God, that love of the whole of humanity. In all capacities he is playing a part and yet keeping the link with the truth which is within. It is all playing. In this way one will have to learn to play a part.

The further one advances in the spiritual path, the more one will have to learn to play the part. When it is said that the twelve apostles, after the blessing came upon them, were able to speak all the languages, it was playing the part. From that moment they learned to answer the question of each, in his own language and his evolution.

That inspiration is the playing of the part.

And about the word of honor, there is Harish Chandra's story, very well known in India, and produced as a play. People have never learned to tire of it. And for myself, this was the first drama I saw when I was a child, and it made such an impression that I came home and produced it with the children. But they would not trouble to learn it by heart, so I had to stand behind each child and say his part. The play is very interesting in its ideal, which shows a most high plane.

Harish Chandra was known to be a king who always kept his promise, and there was a discussion going on among the rishis—the great mystics with miraculous power. They discussed this: is there a man who really keeps his promise? They said it exists in the ideal but no such person really exists, till one said, "I know of a king." "Can you give proof?" "Yes, I will." So the rishi went to court.

The king was very surprised to see a monk of such a high order at the court. As a rule they never come to the court. He said, "King, in my need I have come to you." The king said, "Ask anything of me and I will do it." The rishi said, "Do you promise, King?" and he said, "Yes." So he asked him to give his kingdom, and 3000 pounds more. The king said, "Yes, I will do it." So the kingdom was given to this man. Of course it was a great shock to his people and his ministers and his family. He had a queen and a son. He bade farewell and left the country, and his wife and son followed him. It made a great panic. They did not want him to go, for he was a very good king, but it was his promise and this was his last trial and he would not fail to fulfil his promise. They went, and no wealth was taken from the State; and the whole kingdom belonged to this rishi.

The king and queen suffered as they went through the forest without shoes. It was a new experience to them all. And then after six months, when they had suffered, the rishi came again and said, "King, you promised 3000 pounds more." The king said, "No, I have not forgotten. What about it?" The rishi said, "It is just a matter of the word you gave." The king said, "No, I won't take my word back." So they went to a little town, and a rich man made a contract that he would pay 2000 pounds if the queen and their son would serve as domestics in the rich merchant's house. And it was agreed. And the king went with the rishi further to look for 1000 pounds.

They came to another town where at the crematorium they were looking for a tax collector for that place, and they were glad to take Harish Chandra. He did his duty there, and so at last gave the 3000 pounds in gold coins he had promised. Not one word—there was no speaking about it, he tried to forget it. No light was thrown upon his virtue; it was forgotten.

And so Harish Chandra continued life there, while the queen and prince continued their time as servants. They heard insults from the landlady who never knew a queen was serving, doing every kind of work that came along, never saying who they were. And it so happened that the prince was bitten by a serpent. This was the last shock to the queen, for he was their only child, and he passed away.

She had no friends to call upon for the funeral; she had to carry him to another country herself. And when she came to a crematorium, she found Harish Chandra standing at the gate as the tax collector. He saw a sad woman whom he did not recognize. He said, "Woman, have you brought your tax?" She said, "No, I am too poor." He said, "My master does not allow anyone to be cremated here who does not pay the tax."

He recognized his son and the queen, and saw her grief—but he stood firm in his duty. That was his last trial. He could have had his son cremated, but he still stood firm, never speaking to his wife, who did not recognize him. This moved all the spiritual hierarchy and proved his ordeal.

There appeared the same rishi, bringing good tidings that his son should be awakened and his kingdom given back. It was just a trial. All righteous souls are put to the utmost trial, and the greater the soul, the greater the trial. But when they have passed through the trial and have stood firm, the end is nothing but bliss.

*Question: But a promise may be harmful for others and for yourself.*
Answer: That is a different thing, but if that happens it is better to break it and to repent.

*Question: Some man made a promise to help some spiritual movement. After some years he found that instead of helping the cause, of helping God, that society did not help, but held the light back.*
Answer: Discovering the truth, one should not blindly follow one's promise; one has not taken it away by dishonesty, but by realizing wisely that another thing is better.

# XX

# *Justice*

After having acquired refinement of character, the merits and virtues that are needed in life, the personality can be finished by the awakening of the sense of justice. The art of personality makes a statue into a fine specimen of art, but when the sense of justice is awakened, that statue comes to life. For in the sense of justice there is the secret of the soul's unfoldment.

Everyone knows the name of justice, but rarely can there be found someone who really is just by nature, in whose heart the sense of justice has been awakened. What generally happens is that every person claims to be just, though he may be far from being so. The development of the sense of justice lies in unselfishness. One cannot be just and selfish at the same time. The selfish person can be just, but for himself. He has his own law best suited to himself, and he can change it, and his reason will help him to do so in order to suit his own requirements of life.

A spark of justice is to be found in every heart, in every person, whatever be his stage of evolution in life. But the one who loves fairness, he, so to speak, blows on that spark, thus raising it to a flame, in the light of which life becomes more clear to him. There is so much talk about justice, and there is so much discussion about it, there is so much dispute over it; and in the end one will find two persons arguing upon one certain point, and differing with one another, yet both thinking that they are just. Neither of them will admit that the other is as just as himself.

For those who really learn to be just, their first lesson is what Christ taught, "Judge ye not lest ye be judged." One may say, if one will not judge, how will one learn justice? But the one who judges himself can learn justice, not the one who is occupied in judging others. In this life of limitations, if one only explored oneself one would find within oneself so many faults and weaknesses, and when dealing with others, so much unfairness on the part of oneself, that the soul who really wants to learn justice, for him, his own life will prove to be a sufficient object to practice justice.

Then again comes a stage in one's life, a stage of life's culmination, a stage of the soul's fuller development, when justice and fairness rise to such a height that one arrives at the point of being blameless. He has nothing to say against anyone, and if there is anything to say, it is only against himself. And it is from this point that one begins to see the divine justice hidden behind this manifestation. It comes in one's life as a reward bestowed from above, a reward which is as a trust given by God, to see all things appearing as just and unjust in the bright shining light of perfect justice.

* * *

*Question: Is it not very difficult to avoid judging, because in order to become just one has to come to a certain conclusion?* Answer: Yes, but what man generally does is not only that he judges anyone in his mind, but he is very ready to give his judgement out. He is not patient enough to wait and analyze the matter and think about it more. As a rule a person is not only ready to judge, but without any restraint on his part he will express his judgement instantly. He does not think, "Have I the right to judge that person, have I risen to that stage of evolution?" Jesus Christ himself refused to judge, and said, "Whoever is faultless, it is that person's place to accuse or to punish."

That teaches a great lesson, that even in order to learn justice it is not necessary that we should be ready to judge and ready instantly to express our judgement, our opinion. The idea of the Sufis—who see in every form the divine form, in every heart the divine shrine—for them to judge anyone, whatever be his position, his action, his condition, is in the first place against their religion, which is their respectful attitude toward everyone. And in this manner they develop that philosophy which has been learned by them as intellectuality.

*Question: Does the fact of not blaming others mean that one does not see their faults any more, that we are above seeing them?*
Answer:    No. In the first place, it is a question of self-restraint or of self-control, of politeness, of kindness, of sympathy, of graciousness; of a worshipful attitude toward God, the creator of all beings, and that all are his children, good or bad. If any person's child happened to be homely in appearance, would it be polite to say before the parents, "Your child is homely"?

Then the father and mother of all beings is there, ever-present, and knows what is going on in every person's heart. When we are ready to judge and express our opinion against his creatures, with their faults and their merits before us, it is certainly against the artist who made them, and not behind his back, but [in his presence]. It would not be difficult to feel the presence of God everywhere, if we only were conscious of it.

Besides this, it is not that we only judge impartially the faults and merits of people—it is always our favor and disfavor which is connected with it. Our favor is always inclined to see the merit, our disfavor to see the fault. Is there any person, however great, without a fault? Any person, however wicked, without a merit? Then if we see more faults, it means that we close our heart to a favorable attitude, and we open to that attitude which is unfavorable in order to criticize that person.

Now the other question: are we above seeing them? Yes, there comes a time, after a continual practice of this virtue, when we see the reason behind every fault that appears to us in anyone we meet in our life. We see the reason behind, and we become more tolerant, more forgiving. For instance, there is a person who is ill, who is creating disturbance in his atmosphere by crying or weeping or shouting. It disturbs us, and we say, "How terrible, how bad, how annoying, what a bad nature that person has." It is not the nature, it is the illness. If we looked from a different point of view, it is the reason that makes us tolerant, which can give rise to that forgiveness, the only essence of God, which can be found in the human heart.

*Question: If death as we understand it is not necessary, what is the alternative?*
Answer: Change. Life is change. What we call death is our impression of that change. It is change just the same. And if life is a change, then death is only a change of life.

# XXI

# *Ear-Training*

The art of personality is like the art of music: it wants ear-training and voice-culture. To a person who knows life's music, the art of personality comes naturally, and it is unmusical of a soul, not only inartistic, when it shows the lack of this art in its personality. When one looks at every soul as a note of music and learns to recognize what note it is, flat or sharp, or high or low, and what pitch it belongs to, then he becomes the knower of souls and he just knows how to deal with everybody.

In his own actions, in his own speech, he shows the art. He harmonizes with the rhythm of the atmosphere, with the tone of the person, with the theme of the moment. To become refined is to become musical; it is the musical in soul who is artistic in his personality. When a word is spoken in a different tone, the same word changes its meaning. A word spoken at the proper moment, and held back at the moment when it should not be expressed, completes the music of life.

It is a continual inclination to produce beauty which helps one to develop art in personality. It is amusing how readily man feels inclined to learn the outer refinement, and how slow many souls are found to be to develop that beauty of personality inwardly. It must be remembered that the outer manner is meaningless if it is not prompted by the inner impulse toward beauty.

How pleased God is with man can be learned from the story of Indra, the king of Paradise, at whose court

*Gandharvas* sing and *Upsaras* dance. When interpreted in plain words, this means that God is the essence of beauty. It is his love of beauty which has caused him to express his own beauty in manifestation. And he is pleased when he sees beauty in his manifestation, for it is his desire fulfilled in the objective world.

It is amusing sometimes to watch how a good manner annoys someone who is proud of his bad manner. He will call it shallow because his pride is hurt by the sight of something which he has not got—as the one whose hand does not reach the grapes upon the tree says at his failure that the grapes are sour. And to some it is too fine to become refined, just as many will not like good music and are quite satisfied with the popular music. And many even become tired of good music, for it seems foreign to their nature. As it is not a merit to become unmusical, so it is not wise to turn against refinement. One must only try and develop beauty, trusting that the beauty is the depth of one's soul, and its expression in whatever form is the sign of the soul's unfoldment.

* * *

*Question: What is the difference between individuality and personality?*
Answer: Individuality is the consciousness of the soul of its oneness, in spite of its various possessions with which it still identifies. And that individuality can be seen in the child who says, "No, I do not want this toy, I want another toy." The moment it says "I," it becomes conscious of an individuality in spite of having the different organs of the body and different thoughts, and in spite of knowing that this is my hand, this is my foot, this is my head. One sees one's various parts and yet has the tendency of attributing to oneself all the different parts, still realizing that "I am one." It is the realization that in spite of being many, I am

one. In plain words, I am composed of many aspects. Personality is a development, an improvement of an individuality. When an individual becomes a person, that beauty which is hidden in an individual, which is divine, develops itself, and it is the development of that beauty which is personality—what we express of ourselves as an improvement to what we are.

*Question: If a child does not show a desire for beauty, can one teach the beauty, or can beauty not be taught?*
Answer: If the child does not show an inclination toward beauty, it is only that something is closed in him. It does not mean that the beauty is missing there; in no soul, however wicked or stupid it might seem, [is beauty missing]; the beauty is still hidden there. And it is our trust and confidence in the greatness of the soul which will help us to draw out that beauty; in some sooner and some later, but some day that which is hidden must come out.

Only the difficulty is for everyone to have patience; we have not patience enough, that is the difficulty. The lack of beauty in some people strikes us so hard that we lose our patience, and become pessimistic, and try to run away from them. In doing so we encourage them to become still worse. But if we had the patience to bear it, to endure it, and trust that in every soul there is a goodness and a beauty somewhere hidden: with patience we could explore it and dig it out. Some day or other we shall succeed.

This brings one to the belief in God. If once one believes that God is the father, then fatherhood teaches us that every child has the heritage of the father. It is not only a philosophy, it is a religion, a moral; and by trusting in the divine beauty in every person, we at the same time develop that beauty in ourselves, automatically, because we have the belief. It will not develop when one thinks, "I have that beauty, but another person has not got it." So many persons think, "I have it," instead of forgetting ourselves and thinking that it could be found one day in the other person, if only we had patience to wait. As soon as we think, "Here is someone who is lacking beauty; away, away from him! He has not got what I have," we show pride and lock the door which otherwise could have been kept open for us to toil and work. And it is a weakness to turn our backs to anyone who might seem lacking that beauty which we expect. It is the opening of the heart to every soul, whatever their state of evolution, which alone will inspire the heart with that beauty, and by opening to that beauty one will find it coming to life.

*Question: Where does the quality of conceit come from, and why is it difficult to conquer?*
Answer: It is such a difficult thing to conquer, and it is almost impossible to get rid of. The reason is that where there is a light there is a shadow; there will be darkness as a contrast. So is conceit; it is an attribute of the ego. We call it that because it is the intoxication of the ego. The soberness of the ego may be called divine vanity. The intoxication of the ego is the conceit of man. It is so subtle. The word vanity has been used in a very ordinary sense of the word, and there being no equivalent word, it is very difficult to express it in any other way. Just like *vairagya*, indifference and independence—*kibria*, for the divine vanity. But if plainly explained, it is that satisfaction of God which he wanted to derive by this manifestation. But it is again not the satisfaction of the ignorant soul which makes him conceited. Only when satisfaction is in its proper place, then it is the greatest virtue. Sin and virtue are only the changes of place. It is the inspiration which its own beauty gives which causes the peacock to dance.

*Question: Where does conceit begin?*
Answer: No doubt conceit begins wherever there is comparison. Therefore, even to a small extent, it begins in

the angelic sphere, and also in the *jinn* sphere. It completes itself in the human sphere, where it shows itself to the utmost. But really speaking, the understanding of vanity is the most enjoyable vision of life's phenomena. What the Sufi calls "wine" is the pleasure that he derives from that phenomenon. As soon as this phenomenon is disclosed to his soul, and he sees different actions in life, nothing disappoints him, but everything gives him a wonderful joy, and offers him such amusement that it is almost like a drink. That is what Omar Khayyam calls wine. "Amuse yourself, and by seeing the phenomena of life get above the worries and anxieties that come from self-pity." Always you will find the seers, the most evolved seers, amusing themselves with life. Therefore, they are pleasant to speak with, pleasant in their atmosphere and pleasant in every [way]. When the self is forgotten then there is no worry. Worry comes from fear. What is fear made of? The clouds of ignorance. Life will break up the clouds. One who wishes to be happy can find a thousand things to amuse oneself with and be happy. And if one wants to sorrow over things, one will find a million things to sorrow over.

*Question: How about living worrying about others?*
Answer: By worrying about them, we do not help them.

# XXII

# *Attitude*

A friendly attitude expressed in sympathetic thought, speech, and deed is the principal thing in the art of personality. There is a limitless scope to show this attitude, and however much the personality is developed in this direction it is never too much. Spontaneity, the tendency of giving, giving that which is dear to one's heart: in this one shows the friendly attitude.

Life in the world has its numberless obligations toward friend and foe, toward the acquaintance and the stranger. One can never do too much to be conscientious of one's obligations in life and do everything in one's power in fulfilling them. To do more than one's due is perhaps beyond the power of every man, but in doing what one ought to do one does accomplish one's life's purpose.

Life is an intoxication, and the effect of this intoxication is negligence. The Hindu words *dharma* and *adharma*, religiousness and irreligiousness, both signify one's duty in life to be *dharma*, and the neglect of the same is *adharma*. The one who is not conscientious of his obligations in life toward every being he comes in contact with is indeed irreligious.

Many will say that we try to do our best, but we do not know what it is; or, we do not know what is our due or how we are to find out what is really our due and what is not. No one in this world can teach what is anyone else's due, and what is not. It is for every soul to know for himself by being conscientious of his obligations. And the more conscientious he is, the more obligations he will find to fulfil, and there will be no end to them. Nevertheless, in this continual strife which might seem a loss to him in the beginning, in the end is the gain. For he who is wide awake will come face to face with his Lord.

The man who neglects his duty to his fellow man, absorbed in life's intoxication, his eyes certainly will become dazzled and his mind exhausted before the presence of God. It does not mean that any soul will be deprived of the divine vision. It only means that the soul who has not learned to open his eyes wide enough will have the vision of God before him while his eyes are closed. All virtues come from a wide outlook on life; all understanding comes from the keen observation of life. Nobility of soul, therefore, is signified in the broad attitude that man takes in life.

\* \* \*

*Question: How can one work on personality unconsciously?*
Answer: The best thing is to develop in one's nature love for beauty, and that can be developed by admiration of beauty. Beauty's best expression is in human nature. And if we learn to appreciate and admire the beauty of human nature, and we are impressed by all we admire, then by all with which we come into contact, that becomes our property. In that way we can make a beautiful collection of what every person has to offer. It is the critical tendency and the lack of appreciation which keeps the personality back from progress. Because the best opportunity that life offers is to get all the good from every person; that opportunity is lost by seeing the bad side and overlooking the good. But if we saw some good in every person, we could take and collect it, and in this way we develop the love of art. It is just like a man going from here to China and different countries, and finding the best pieces of art,

collecting them and then making a museum, such as the Musée Guimet.[19] When in a material way a person can do this, in a higher way it can also be done.

By taking the good of a person, one does not rob that person of the good. We only appreciate it and come closer to that person, and by that become richer and richer with beauty. And beauty so collected in the end results in a beautiful personality. There is never an end: in the most ordinary person there is something to be found, something we can learn from every person, if we only had the desire to appreciate and find good in that person. And if the good were hidden, to try and draw it out. And to draw out good from another person, what does it want? It wants currency. What is currency? Goodness in oneself. Give that currency, and it gives back that which is hidden there.

*Question: How can a soul always know its duty? May not overscrupulosity bring confusion of thought and wrong action?* Answer: Over-goodness or over-kindness or over-lovingness—"over" is always bad. But what generally is the case, what one always finds, is the intoxication. Soberness is very difficult. The life has its effect of intoxication upon every soul—on a saint, a sage, on everyone. That intoxication is overwhelming; it keeps a person back from a clear understanding. And therefore, however far advanced a person, even in the spiritual life, he can never be too sure of himself, that he will not be taken up in this intoxication: because he is breathing it in with everything he smells or tastes or hears, which veils everything else. Therefore, one cannot be too conscientious.

For instance, such a case may be found in the mind of a person who is unbalanced, who already has a confusion. He does not know whether he has done wrong or right. I am not talking about that person at all. That person I do not call conscientious. That person I call confused. He does not know what he is doing. A conscientious person does not discuss it, only he is continually wide awake, and he always asks, "Where should I have done something?" or "Why have I not done it?", in every situation or condition. But he does not confuse himself. He just does what he thinks right. And if it happens that it turns out to be wrong, the next time it will be right. The one who wants to do right will do wrong once, twice, thrice, but in the end he will do right, because he wants to do right.

*Question: Will you please tell us if it is possible to guard against the moments of* kemal *in which accidents may happen?* Answer: No, one must not trouble about it. Because the thought of accident attracts accident. It is best not to trouble about it. But in order to avoid such accident the best thing is to keep tranquil, because all accidents come when the tranquillity of mind is disturbed. And if one keeps one's mind in a proper balance, no accident will come. An accident always follows the broken rhythm of mind. When the mind has lost its rhythm, then there is an accident. But you may say, when a person has a motorcar accident, is it his fault? Not the fault of the chauffeur? But the answer may be: maybe it is the fault of the chauffeur, or maybe it is his own fault, in that his mind has upset the chauffeur, or someone else's. The accident might come from another motorcar, and also be reflected by his mind. No one can blame the other because they do not know. An accident is not natural. It is something unnatural, and something undesirable. For instance, a false note or lack of rhythm was not meant by the composer. He did not mean it. And when a person plays it, it is a mistake, it is not a desire.

# XXIII

# *Reconciliation*

Any efforts made in developing the personality or character must not be for the sake of proving oneself superior to others, but in order to become more agreeable to those around one and to those with whom one comes in contact.

Reconciliation is not only the moral of the Sufi, but is the sign of the Sufi. This virtue is not learned and practiced easily, for it needs not only good will but wisdom. The great talent of the diplomat is to bring about such results as are desirable, with agreement. Disagreement is easy; among the lower creation one sees it so often. What is difficult is agreement, for it wants a wider outlook, which is the true sign of spirituality. Narrowness of outlook makes the horizon of man's vision small. That person cannot easily agree with another.

There is always a meeting ground for two people, however much they differ in their thought. But the meeting ground may be far off, and man is not always willing to take the trouble of going far enough if that were required in order to make an agreement. Very often his patience does not allow him to go far enough where he could meet with another. In an ordinary case, what happens is that everyone wants another to meet him in the same place where he is standing. There is no desire on his part to move from the place where he stands.

I do not mean that a person, in order to become a real Sufi, must give up his idea in order to meet in agreement with another. And there is no benefit in always being lenient to every thought that comes from another; there is no benefit in always erasing our own idea from our own heart. But that is not reconciliation. The one who is able to listen to another is the one who will make another listen to him. It is the one who easily will agree with another who will have the power of making another easily agree with him. Therefore, in doing so, one gains in spite of the apparent loss which might sometimes occur. When man is able to see from one's own point of view as well as from the point of view of another, he has complete vision and clear insight. He, so to speak, sees with both eyes.

No doubt friction produces light, but light is the agreement of the atoms. For stimulus to thought, if two people have their own ideas and argue upon their different ideas, it does not matter so much. But when a person argues for the sake of argument, the argument becomes his game. He has no satisfaction in reconciliation. Words provide the means of disagreement. Reasons become the fuel for that fire. But wisdom is when the intelligence is pliable; it understands all things, the wrong of the right and the right of the wrong.

The soul who arrives at perfect knowledge has risen above right and wrong. He knows them and yet knows not. He can say much, and yet, what can he say? Then it becomes easy for him to reconcile with each and all.

There is a story that two Sufis met after many years, having travelled along their own lines. They were glad to meet each other after many years' separation, for the reason that they were both mureeds of the same murshid. One said to the other, "Tell me please your life's experience." "After all this time's study and practice of Sufism, I have learned one thing: how to reconcile with another, and I can do it very well now. Will you please tell me what you have learned?" The other one said, "After all this time's study and practice of Sufism, I have learned to know how to master life, and all that there is in this world is for me, and

I am the master. All that happens, happens by my will."
There came the murshid whose mureeds they both
were. And both spoke of their experience during this
journey. The murshid said, "Both of you are right. In the
case of the first, it was self-denial in the right sense of the
word which enabled him to reconcile with others. In the
case of the other, there was no more of his will left; if there
was any, it was the will of God."

# Endnotes

1. *Fusus al-Hikam*, chapter on Adam.

2. Inayat Khan, following the custom of his day, used the masculine pronoun when referring to both sexes. He also often used inclusive language, such as "one" or "we." This volume has not been edited to be gender inclusive. Please see Preface for an explanation of this decision. Also, see the Appendix for a version of this lecture edited to be gender inclusive.

3. The month of Ramadan observed by Muslims.

4. *Mureed* is the Sufi word for an initiate; *murshid* is the word for spiritual teacher.

5. *A Sufi Message of Spiritual Liberty*, the first book of Inayat Khan's teachings to appear in the West, was published in Russian and English in 1914.

6. A book of sayings of Inayat Khan, many of which were derived from his personal notebooks, first published in 1923.

7. Probably referring to the *Masnavi*, the great work of Rumi's last years. A recent article has revealed that Jelal-ud-Din Rumi is currently the most widely published poet in the United States of America.

8. See *The Hand of Poetry*, Omega Publications, 1993, for some of Inayat Khan's lectures on the Persian Sufi poets.

9. The second book of sayings of Inayat Khan, first published in 1926.

10. Luke xxii.36.

11. Ed. note: The idea that St. Paul assembled the New Testament three hundred years after the time of Christ appears several times in the teaching of Pir-o-Murshid Inayat Khan. This historical error must have resulted from something he was told by one of his followers.

12. An early editor added, "when it was entering Belgium." This refers to the First World War.

13. For a much fuller treatment of all these terms, see the book *The Soul: Whence and Whither?*, edited from lectures given in the same summer as those in the present book. A new edition of that book, following the same editorial guidelines as the present volume, is planned for the near future.

14. *Purusha* is a Sanskrit word indicating the soul as passive.

15. The shorthand record of the question is incomplete. Another record reads, "A, who had a body and matter that had passed out of the body of another person, B, and gone into the body of A, would that person, A, feel connection with the person, B?"

16. A classic of Persian literature by Firdausi, a history of the kings of that country.

17. A book by Inayat Khan, published earlier in 1923. It contains lectures describing the ways in which sound is used in mystical exercises.

18. Genesis III.17-19.

19. A museum of Asian art in Paris, where Pir-o-Murshid Inayat Khan occasionally lectured.

# Appendix

*The first chapter is repeated here, having been further edited to be gender inclusive. Masculine pronouns and the noun "man" have been replaced with the gender inclusive principles already present in the talks of Pir-o-Mursid Hazrat Inayat Khan, using the plural, "one," and "the human being." This allows the reader to sense the difference in both rhythm and flavor of the use of inclusive language, while the main text honors the author's request that his words not be changed. Readers are, of course, free to substitute gender inclusive language as they read through the text, and the principles illustrated in this example may be helpful in that regard.*

# *Will Power*

Will power plays a great part in character building, and will power becomes feeble when one yields to every little tendency, inclination, and fancy one has. When one fights against every little fancy and tendency and inclination, one learns to fight with oneself, and in this way one develops will power. When once one's inclinations, fancies, and tendencies have grown stronger than one's will power, then one experiences in one's life several enemies existing in one's own self, and one finds it difficult to combat them; for inclinations, fancies, and tendencies, when powerful, do not let will power work against them. If there is anything like self-denial, it is this practice; and by this practice, in time, one attains to a power which may be called mastery over oneself.

In small things of everyday life, one neglects this consideration for the reason that one thinks, "These are my tendencies, my fancies, my inclinations, and by respecting them I respect myself; by considering them I consider myself." But one forgets that what one calls "me" is not oneself. It is what wills that is oneself. Therefore, in the Christian prayer it is taught "Thy will be done," which means, "Thy will, when it works through me, will be done"; in other words, "My will, which is thy will, will be done." It is this illusion of muddling one's possession with oneself that creates all illusion and keeps one from self-realization.

Life is a continual battle. We struggle with things which are outside of ourselves; we give a chance to the foes who exist in our own being. Therefore, the first thing necessary in life is to make peace for the time being with the outside world in order to prepare for the war which is to be fought within ourselves. Once peace is made within, we will gain by that sufficient strength and power to be used in the struggle of life within and without.

Self-pity is the worst poverty. When people say "I am" with pity, before they have said anything more, they have diminished what they are to half, and what is said further diminishes them totally. Nothing more is left of them afterwards. There is so much in the world which we can pity and which it would be right for us to take pity on. But if we have no time free from our own self, we cannot give our mind to the condition of others in the world. Life is one long journey, and the more we have left ourselves behind, the further we have progressed toward the goal. Verily, when the false self is lost, the true self is discovered.

\* \* \*

*Question: Why do we find satisfaction in self-pity?*
Answer: The reason is that by nature we find satisfaction in love. And when we are confined to ourselves, we begin to love ourselves; for our limitations we have self-pity. But therefore, the love of self always brings dissatisfaction, because the self is made to love, and, when we love, the first condition of love is that we forget our self. We cannot love another person by loving our self at the same time. The condition of love is to forget oneself; then one knows how to love. If one says, "Give me a sixpence and I will give you a shilling," that is another kind of love.

*Question: Do you mean by the false self, the ego?*
Answer: Yes, by the false self I mean the false ego, the deluding

ego, someone who has disguised the self as the ego. The reason is that the human being's ego is the false ego. What is the ego? It is that line which connects God and the human being, that line, one end of which is the human being, the other is God. Therefore, that end which is the human being's ego is false, because the human being has covered it with the false ego. The ego is true, it is divine, it cannot be anything else. But the human being covers it with illusions and calls it "me," "myself." When that wrong conception is broken by knowledge, love, wisdom, or meditation, then it is just like the clouds being broken which cover the sun, and the true ego comes out, the only ego there is.

*Question: Is it easy to say, "Thy will be done"?*
Answer: There are two ways of looking at it: the way of the master and of the saint. The way of the saint is, "Thy will be done"; the way of the master is, "My will be done." In the end both things become one. But to say, "Thy will be done" is a resignation.

*Question: Is it possible for an ego to come on earth and never be covered by clouds of illusion?*
Answer: No, the beauty is to come out of that illusion. If one came wise, there would be no joy in coming out of it. The joy is in the unveiling.
    The question is, what is the ego? It is the ego in us which says "I." It is that ego which says, "This is mine." When people say, "I am sorry," what is it in them that says "I am sorry"? It is their ego, not their hand, their eye, their ear.

*Question: The difference between the false and real ego is the difference between selfishness and unselfishness?*
Answer: Yes, the result of the manifestation of the real ego is unselfishness. It is a natural outcome of it, and the more one is absorbed in the false ego, the more selfish that person is.

*Question: To say "I am sorry" is an act of compassion. How then can the false ego say this?*
Answer: The real ego does not know sorrow; it is happiness. We long for happiness because our true being is happiness. God is happiness. There are many people who do not long for God, but

they long for happiness. It is the same thing. For instance, an atheist says there is no God, but that person longs for happiness. God is happiness.

*Question: What really is the character?*
Answer: Character is, so to speak, a picture with lines and colors we make within ourselves. And it is wonderful to see how the tendency of character building springs up from childhood, just like one sees the instinct of building a nest in a bird. The little child begins to note everything in the grown-up people and begins to adopt all that seems to it best: the word, the manner, the movement, the idea, everything that it grasps from the grown-up, whatever seems to its own mind best. It attracts it, and it builds, so to speak, a building which is its character. It is being built all through life.

By this we understand that when a person is absorbed in the self, one has no time to see the other; then there is no other. But when one forgets oneself, one has the time to see here and there and add naturally to one's character. So the character is built. One need not make an effort in building the character if one only forgets oneself. For instance, if the great actors and actresses, with great qualifications, do not forget themselves, they cannot act; they may have all capability. So musicians, when they cannot forget at the time they are playing, they cannot perform music to their satisfaction. So with the poet, the artist. Think then that the whole work of building oneself and everything else all depends on how much one is able to forget oneself, which is the key to the whole of life, material and spiritual, and to success. It seems such a simple thing, and yet it is so difficult.

The wonderful thing is that during my travels, whenever I have met very great people in anything, art, science, thought, religion, philosophy, whatever be their work, I have found that they have touched that greatness with this quality, the quality of forgetting themselves. Always, everywhere it is the same. And I have again seen people with great qualifications, but they remember themselves so much that they cannot do the best with their lives. I have known a vina player, who tried so much, playing his instrument, for six, nine hours a day. But whenever he used to go in the assembly, he became so nervous because he thought of himself. And all the impressions of the people would fall upon him. He would take his instrument and cover it and run away. He never had a chance of being great, even with all his qualifications.

Self-confidence is a great thing, but forgetting oneself is greater still.

I have seen Sarah Bernhardt. She was singing a very simple song, the National Anthem of France. When she came on the stage she won every person there. At that time she was the nation; with that sentiment in the feeling and the words, she was France at that time, because of her concentration.

# Index